# ADVANCE REVIEWS

"At a time when so much thinking about politics, culture, and social change seems irrevocably stuck in the unproductive ruts of a failed conventional wisdom, Craig K. Comstock reminds us that here, too, innovation is possible—and necessary. *Better Ways to Live* challenges the reader to break out of the unthinking assumptions of our era into a wider world; it's hard to think of anything more timely"

> —JOHN MICHAEL GREER, author of *Retrotopia* and *After Progress: Reason and Religion at the End of the Industrial Age*

"*Better Ways to Live* is about social inventions that are working and about new challenges that call for such inventions. In short, it's about things we can do even in the worst of times. I've rarely seen a book that marches so resolutely up to the challenges and proposes a way to build, alongside the necessary protest. Here is social invention at every scale, from the community up to the globe, what already exists and what we can do."

> —THOM HARTMANN, host of *The Big Picture*, on national TV; radio host; and author of many books.

"Craig Comstock has always been ahead of the curve, from selling Kennedy aides on the idea that became the Peace Corps to initiating some of the early U.S.-Soviet citizen dialogue initiatives at the height of the Cold War. *Better Ways* is a lovely collection of conversations and reflections on what it means to create a better world, in small and large ways, in the process crossing some of the boundaries that isolate and separate us. I always learn some powerful lessons when I read Craig's books."

> —PAUL ROGAT LOEB, author of *Soul of a Citizen* and *The Impossible Will Take A Little While*

"In dark times for this country, it's good to be reminded of just how many people are trying to do good and decent things. A small fraction of those folks come to life in these pages, and they will hearten you!"

—BILL McKIBBEN, founder of 350.org, author of *Oil and Honey: The Education of an Unlikely Activist* and of the first general book to call attention to climate change, *The End of Nature*

# BOOKS & OTHER MAJOR PUBLICATIONS
*by the author*

## THE GRATITUDE TRILOGY (2015–17)
*(Each book is self-contained and may be read apart from the other two; what the trilogy shares is an attitude applied to very different subjects.)*

### Gift of Darkness
*Growing Up in Occupied Amsterdam*

### Enlarging Our Comfort Zones
*A Life of Unexpected Destinations*

### Better Ways to Live
*Honoring Social Inventors, Exploring New Challenges*

As the name of a trilogy, "gratitude" may sound goody-goody. It's not. It can be hard to articulate gratitude after the habit of complaint, of self-doubt, of disappointment, of denial. What does it mean to be grateful for what we have and can do? From one point of view, that of perpetual striving, being satisfied seems almost dangerous; it can seem like giving up. From another point of view, that of this trilogy, noticing and specifying things for which you are grateful is an act of creativity, of grace.

In this trilogy, Book One expresses my gratitude for a friend being willing to revisit the trauma of his adolescence under Nazi rule, along with his own gratitude for surviving that period (*Gift of Darkness*). Book Two is full of gratitude for the life that I've been able to live, for the opportunity to do and experience things richer than I ever expected (*Enlarging Our Comfort Zones*). Book Three is a celebration of social invention, and a look at challenges currently arising (*Better Ways to Live*).

## EARLIER WORKS
*(in chronological order)*

***Worse Than Futile,*** *the Loyalty Provision of the National Defense Education Act,* with Foreword by Senator John F. Kennedy (published by *The Harvard Crimson,* 1960)

***Sanctions for Evil,*** *Sources of Social Destructiveness* (with Nevitt Sanford; published by Jossey-Bass, Inc., 1971; then by Beacon Press, 1972)

***Faculty Development in a Time of Retrenchment,*** a report on behalf of the Group from Human Development in Higher Education, of which the author was a member (Change Magazine Press, 1974)

***Citizen Summitry,*** *Keeping the Peace When It Matters Too Much to be Left to Politicians* (with Don Carlson, published by Tarcher, 1986)

***Securing Our Planet,*** *How to Succeed When Threats are Too Risky and There's Really No Defense* (with Don Carlson, published by Tarcher, 1986)

***Global Partners,*** *Citizen Exchange with the Soviet Union* (Ark Communications Institute, 1987)

***The Elmwood Quarterly*** (founded and edited in 1992–93)

# Better Ways to *Live*

## Honoring Social Inventors, Exploring New Challenges

### CRAIG K. COMSTOCK

WILLOW PRESS    WILLOW PRESS    ASHLAND, OREGON

*Better Ways to Live: Honoring Social Inventors, Exploring New Challenges*
*by* Craig K. Comstock

Published in 2017 by Willow Press, Ashland, Oregon
www.willowpressbooks.com

Design and copyediting: Book Savvy Studio, Ashland, Oregon
Artwork on section dividers: *Shield for Angie* by Craig K. Comstock

Quote from Alexis de Tocqueville on the back cover: A less epigrammatic but
perhaps more faithful version is found in the 2004 Library of America edition
of *Democracy in America* (as translated by Arthur Goldhammer, on page 275):
*"That nothing is more prodigal of wonders than the art of being free is a truth that
cannot be repeated too often. But nothing is harder than the apprenticeship
of liberty."* —Alexis de Toqueville

**Publisher's Cataloging-in-Publication**
***(Provided by Quality Books, Inc.)***

Comstock, Craig, 1939- author.
    Better ways to live! : honoring social inventors,
    exploring new challenges / Craig K. Comstock. -- First
    edition.
        pages cm -- (The gratitude trilogy ; book 3)
        Includes bibliographical references.
        ISBN 978-0-9967044-1-0

    1. Social movements. 2. Social change. 3. Social
    reformers. 4. Nuclear warfare--Social aspects.
    5. Global warming--Social aspects. 6. Consumption
    (Economics)--Social aspects.   I. Title. II. Series:
    Comstock, Craig, 1939- Gratitude trilogy ; bk. 3.

    HM881.C645 2017              303.48'4
                                 QBI17-900001

ISBN: 978-0-9967044-1-0

10 9 8 7 6 5 4 3 2 1

First Edition

# DEDICATION

This book is dedicated to
social inventors who have already
made a contribution, and to those who will do so,
who may meanwhile benefit from a little
encouragement and some models; in particular,
to people who will take on the challenges
sketched in the latter part of this book.

# Contents

## SOCIAL JUSTICE

## ECONOMIC INITIATIVES

## WORLD POLITICS

## GLOBAL WARMING

## TOUGH TIMES SCENARIOS

# Contents

## DIFFERENT KINDS OF SPIRIT

# HONOR ROLL OF SOCIAL INVENTORS

The following people in this book started something, or noticed the need to do so, or wrote about social inventions.

All are (or were) contemporaries of the author, as friends, sources, mentors, or writers, except for a few who are historical and indicated with an asterisk. Italics indicate people whom I met in southern Oregon.

*Zoe Alowan*
Kevin Anderson
Dan Ariely
Stephen Bachelor
Carolyn Baker
*Denise Baxter*
*Anne Bellegia*
Lester Brown
Brad Burge
Fyodor Burlatsky
William BC Crandall
Rick Doblin
Tom Engelhardt
Jim Fadiman
David Fridley
*Jeff Golden*
Clive Hamilton
Richard Heinberg
Adam Hochschild
Rob Hopkins
*Chris Jagger*
Thomas Jefferson*
*Bill Kauth*

*Jun Po Denis Kelly Roshi*
John F. Kennedy
Martin Luther King, Jr.
Eli Kintisch
*Ron Kurtz*
*Leslie Lanes*
*Bill MacMillan*
Bill McKibben
Ralph Metzner
Michael Mithoefer
John U. Monro
Michael I. Norton
*James di Properzio*
Franklin D. Roosevelt*
*Kim Shelton*
*Marion Spadone*
Sharon Tennison
Henry David Thoreau*
Julienne Travers
*Cara Walsh*
Francis Weller
*Mark Yaconelli*
*Peter Young*

# Better Ways to Live

## Honoring Social Inventors, Exploring New Challenges

# Introduction

Everybody knows what physical inventions are. These objects are ubiquitous, and many can be handled in some way while being used (for example, a mobile phone); set in a room (a television); or even entered (a passenger jet). Another illustration of physical invention is the immediate power we receive from a wall outlet, thanks to the discovery of alternating current electricity.

In contrast, *social* inventions are a set of arrangements or practices, sometimes codified in rules, which govern the way we live.[1]

New ways of doing things are often disruptive, but once accepted, once widely adopted, they quickly become almost invisible—and it feels amazing that people ever behaved otherwise. On the other hand, when we travel and are dropped into a different set of social inventions, we may experience culture shock.

Physical inventions can often be patented, after which they receive legal protection. Social inventions, because they are ways of living, are as hard for us to grasp as for a fish to grasp water. They are the medium in which we live.

What are some examples of social invention? A good place to begin is with a document drafted by Thomas Jefferson.[2] *The Declaration of Independence* proceeds as if it's "self-evident" that "all men are created equal," that they have "inalienable rights," among which are "life, liberty, and the pursuit of happiness," that governments derive their powers "from the consent of the governed," that "the people" have the right "to institute new government."

Whatever the value of pretending these ideas were "self-evident," their assertion by what had been a colony, was revolutionary. And while the declaration was said to be justified by "a long train of abuses and usurpations," as Jefferson went on to say, "absolute Despotism" had been the rule for many people throughout history, with the standard language for this arrangement being "the divine right of kings." But "consent of the governed"? Here was a cascade of major social inventions.

However, a social invention can be much smaller, less risky, than a declaration of independence, and this book starts with examples from my own town where we are fortunate to have residents who put forward ideas of better ways to live—along with many others who are willing to try them and, in many cases, to adopt them.

Descriptions of contemporary social inventions and their innovators appear in the first few sections of this collection of articles and interviews (and, in a few cases, in later chapters). Since social inventions can't be patented, they can be adopted anywhere, taking advantage of our freedom to create voluntary organizations and, to some extent, to influence the relevant governments.

At the front of this volume is an honor roll of social inventors who appear in these pages and who are among the many "champions" of ways of living found in this country and abroad, both past and present. Apart from Jefferson, Thoreau, and FDR, all of the chapters herein are about people who are (or were) my contemporaries, in some cases people with whom I have worked (such as Jun Po Denis Kelly Roshi, then-Senator John F. Kennedy, then-Dean John U. Monro, Nevitt Sanford[3]), been in a men's group with (Jeff Golden, Bill Kauth, Ron Kurtz), or who have appeared on my television show (Denise Baxter, Anne Bellegia, Chris Jagger, Leslie

Lanes, Bill MacMillan, James di Properzio, Sharon Tennison, Pete Young).

The idea of social invention, while less than widespread, is not new. In 1981 the presidential address of the American Sociological Association was called "Social Inventions for Solving Human Problems." While discussing first-hand studies of cooperatives in Spain and agricultural research and development organizations in Latin America, William Foote Whyte defined social inventions as "a new element in organization structure," as "new sets of procedures," as "a new policy in action," and as "a new role." When anthropologists study a culture, much of what they study are sets of social inventions, most of which have been made long before.

 If a considerable amount of what's not a set of physical inventions is the social kind, what is the point of focusing on the latter? Here we return to the fact that while physical inventions are palpable (even if we don't know how they work), most social inventions become invisible, as easily forgotten as the unconscious. We know the unconscious is there, but by definition it is not accessible to our conscious mind, not on the surface.

One of the merits of travel is that the culture in which we grew up, the culture that seems natural, may be revealed as "merely" a set of inventions. Travel enables us to see how other cultures have made different inventions. There are a few people who have recently made a list of possible social inventions, one of whom is Nicholas Albery, who sought ideas from all over the globe and founded a "bank" of these ideas.

However valuable and necessary, ideas are only the first stage of social invention. Each idea needs at least one person who champions it, often in the face of opposition—or at least disinterest. Social inventors are familiar with the observer who first says "Don't waste your time, it's ridiculous." (Or impossible, or irrelevant.) But if the idea gains traction the observer may then say, "We have to stop this before it destroys civilization." And if the champion persists and the idea is really helpful and widely adopted, the same observer might be heard to say, "Well, I thought of this myself, years ago."

While some social inventions are so well seasoned that people can't recall life *without* this way of doing things, others are still in the very first stage—which is noticing that there is a challenge to be met and stumbling toward ways of meeting it. For example, three of our many challenges today are the effects of consumerism, the danger of nuclear war, and the process of global warming.

It seems we have lived so long with nuclear weapons (more than seventy years), that we can just go on threatening one another without any apparent problem. And the severe effects of global warming are thought to be so far in the future that we have time to see how things develop before we react. Both assumptions are understandable but, unfortunately, false (see Chapters 29 and 32). As for consumerism, the Buddha taught that craving leads to suffering, but we have built an economic system around the deliberate amplification of craving and regard this, too, as natural. Are there other ways to live? For examples, see Chapters 24 and 44.

What is depressing to me is less "the state of the world" than a denial of reality, the assumption that mutual nuclear threats can go on forever or that a process attested by many professional scientists from many fields is a "hoax." The situation can also be seen as a set of challenges. It's true that we are facing things at least on the scale of the American Revolution or World War II, but what people did then in response to the threats they were encountering can illustrate what we are capable of as well. As President Reagan used to say, if you open a door and discover a room full of horse turds, perhaps the best response is, "Oh good, there must be a pony in here somewhere."

One difficulty is that some of our challenges now are nearly invisible, or are troubling but do not seem urgent. Ignorance may be bliss for a while, but what about later? Perhaps the first step is to recognize the category of social invention; the second, to have gratitude for the social inventions we already enjoy; and the third, to start inventing. Anybody can take part.

Around 80 percent of the following chapters are drawn from articles previously published online, mainly by *The Huffington Post* and also by *Op Ed News* and *Alternet*. The other 20 percent are lightly edited transcripts from my television interview show, which was dedicated to "people doing something admirable and not ordinarily seen on TV." Each of the forty-four chapters centers around a social inventor who changed the way we live or, as a first step, envisioned another way of living or drew attention to a challenge that requires a social invention.

*Better Ways to Live* is dedicated to those social inventors who have already made contributions and to others who may become inspired. The game of building culture is one that many people have played, obviously far beyond those honored in this book, and one which can be joined by a wide range of people who have not yet become active.

In order to get outside what is taken for granted, "the way it's always been done," we need to employ every aid to creativity. Used wisely, what a friend calls "mindful molecules" may offer one path, suggesting that perhaps the main danger of psychedelics is trivialization. With an experienced guide and the right intention, what benefits can a healthy person actually expect to enjoy? Chapters 17 and 18 contain surprising answers, along with possible inspiration that these experiences may yield for social inventions.

The culture that we regard as natural was at various times the beneficiary of social inventions that originated in response to severe challenges. While it's not clear that we shall succeed in accomplishing the tasks at hand, a doubt explored by several of the people profiled in this book (Kevin Anderson, Carolyn Baker, Clive Hamilton, Richard Heinberg), later chapters include suggestions about how to live in tough times, and in particular, about spiritual resources that are available, leading us to perhaps the most significant question of all: To what extent, as a society, can we learn—to quote the title of the book by Ram Dass—to "be here now"?

# Community Building

# CHAPTER 1

# The Grace of Social Inventions

It's social inventions that make the difference between an okay town and a great one. Fortunately social inventions aren't restricted; they can be freely reproduced.

Here are seven examples from a town in southern Oregon, which also happens to be on many lists of the best places to retire.[4] Yes, the area has theater, hiking trails, and a river for rafting, but its foremost grace is a rich network of social inventions.

A good place to start is with the sharing of true stories. Once every season an organization called The Hearth sponsors an evening, now attended by hundreds, at which ordinary people tell about episodes from their lives. Each participant gets ten minutes, with live music at the beginning of the evening and at the end, and all proceeds from the $5 tickets are given to a local charity. The most recent theme was "borders." This is a model that could be replicated anywhere. (See Chapter 2.)

This town also has an arts center, where there are open studios that can be visited, a gallery, a community classroom, a ceramics workshop, and walls available for displaying photography. As a result the artists are no longer isolated, they have another venue for their work, and are able to teach kids and their parents. The center is supported by studio rentals, art sales, and grants. (Chapter 4 gives more details.)

An international organization, the Mankind Project, is especially well represented in this area, perhaps because its co-founder lives here. MKP sponsors a "training adventure," which lasts for one very intensive weekend plus an integration series for the attendees when they return home. Among its local activities is a circle of elders. Since "integrity" is a big MKP virtue, when looking for a builder I favored someone who had received the training. (See Chapter 11.)

Some other social inventions resulted from a circle of guys, organized by Bill Kauth, who call themselves "The Relentless Optimists" and still meet weekly. One of their inventions is an annual "Abundance Swap." In the frantic shopping season after Thanksgiving, people are invited to bring items they already have and that they think others might be happy to receive as gifts. After walking around the tables in the cavernous hall where the swap is held, each person can choose anything he or she wants, while somebody else takes what that person brought. Despite the name, it's not the usual swap at which two people exchange items. You give to the community, and select something that catches your eye. (More in Chapter 5.)

Also present in the town, and in a number of other towns in the area, are many "Heart Circles" which are based on a book by an early member of the relentless optimists. Just as The Hearth offers true stories, heart circles support the vulnerability necessary for truth telling.

On the north edge of town is a planned community of separate homes and condominia where retirees can "age in place," rather than disappearing into isolation or going prematurely into a nursing home. The development includes a dining hall, activity rooms, and a bus to take residents to town for shopping.

One more example, which resulted when the plight of returning veterans became evident to a local couple, was the engagement of Michael Meade to lead a workshop where vets were invited to write poems about their experiences. These poems were then read to an audience of around five hundred townspeople. The workshop and evening are the subjects of a documentary film, which is shown nationwide. (Reviewed in Chapter 19.)

Also worthy of mention are a center for restorative justice, a computer-based community bulletin board, a "New Tribes" movement (Chapter 7), a "Peace House," a food co-op, an institute for senior education (Chapter 6), a weekly "ecstatic dance," a major and successful electoral campaign for the exclusion of genetically modified crops, a sustainability center at the local university, and other social inventions.

What did each of these initiatives have in common? A champion and the help of volunteers.

European visitors to the U.S. in the nineteenth century, such as Alexis de Tocqueville, praised the voluntary associations they found here. Any group could form, choose a name, open a bank account, and begin operating without permission from anybody.

In contrast, totalitarian states are organized from the capitol. For example, in the former U.S.S.R. you were supposed to petition the center (as Moscow was called). This rule was broken by a guy I met on a visit to Moscow, Gennady Alferenko, who, in the distant Siberian city of Novosibirsk, had organized an association of dance enthusiasts, and later wrote in the main national newspaper for youth *(Komsomolskaya Pravda)* asking what social needs could be met by volunteer effort—which prompted an outpouring of letters. This was one beginning of civil society in the country that eventually became known as Russia after the fall of the U.S.S.R.. Meanwhile, Gorbachev rewarded Alferenko by putting him in charge of exit visas, which, in turn, led to citizen diplomacy exchanges with the U.S.

We have many freedoms that are sometimes more assumed or bragged about than acted upon, but it is the freedom to start voluntary associations that led to each of these examples above.

# CHAPTER TWO

# What's Your Story?

"They stand up in front of friends and hundreds of strangers and tell personal stories that maybe only a spouse has heard," said Mark Yaconelli, founder of The Hearth, which sponsors an ongoing series of quarterly storytelling events in my Northwestern town. "Some of these tellers unburden themselves of shame and grief that may have been with them for decades."

Meanwhile the audience (240 in church pews on a recent evening) listens respectfully: What they hear is healthier than gossip because it's true, it comes from the person who was involved, and the telling feels brave. I don't know how most of the other people felt, but for me this was a relief from, for example, the innuendos of *Downton Abbey*, where repeatedly a character introduces a topic, then quickly veers away from any direct statement. It was a relief, too, from evasions in my own culture.

The format for The Hearth is simple: Three stories of ten to fifteen minutes each, sandwiched by live music, a break, and more of the same, followed by Yaconelli's spontaneous, brief, and eloquent tying together of the main themes that emerge on that evening. The overall topic one recent night was bullies, and the proceeds from the tickets were donated to a local program that works against bullying. The church, the organizer, and the musicians? All volunteers like the storytellers.

Yaconelli uses storytelling, a revival of an ancient art, as an occasion to build community by giving people an opportunity to be witnessed as they share some precious episode from their own lives—an adventure, a discovery, a shame, a success, a hurt, a joyful occasion. Those who tell stories are not performers doing standup comedy, nor is the occasion as solemn as, well, a church service. These are regular folks: A car salesman, an attorney, a coach, a father, a secretary.

Clothing is informal at these evening gatherings, and the feeling is less an auditorium than a living room that just happens to have grown. In this sense, the event could be called a hearth or a campfire with a microphone. The audience is there not to judge, but to witness, in some cases to identify with.

Clearly, similar evenings of storytelling could be done in any town. Mine has a population of only 20,000. This kind of event does not require an enormous metropolis such as New York City or Los Angeles. Classical Athens was tiny by modern standards, but what it had were traditions, an audience, occasions.

To find storytellers Yaconelli keeps his eye out for regular folks, and people come not to gawk at a show but to hear others who may be like themselves.

The Hearth is also a tribute to transparency. The organizer told me about man with an Irish father and a Puerto Rican mother who as a child was told to suggest he had Mediterranean origins—perhaps Spanish or Italian—as he would intimate by speaking a phrase in one of the latter languages. After not showing up for a couple of events he finally did tell his story, which concluded with his coming out as a Puerto Rican. This was hard for him, but the outcome was a standing ovation.

Often people come to Yaconelli with stories that aren't what they end up telling. He listens for the moment of passion and then asks questions, inviting them to focus on and expand what they really care about. His goal is not "true confessions," but something real and not ordinarily spoken.

Yaconelli started his career as a minister to young people, a subject about which he's written books and given workshops. As his older children finish high school he is shifting his focus to helping people "drop into the heart" and, as a result, feel closer to one another. While he recognizes that "Buddhists have a near monopoly on the concept of compassion," he sees his own faith, Christianity, as "a set of love stories," and wants to encourage love first for the self, then for the family or other small group, for friends, and finally for the larger community.

The Moth,[5] in New York City, is named after the Georgia background of its organizer, who describes how a hole in the screen door would admit moths to the light on summer evenings as friends talked about their lives. Apart from The Moth, and its satellites in several other big cities, San Francisco has a storytelling organization called Porchlight, run by two women and held in a big bar. And while the Moth has a large staff, Yaconelli points out that storytelling is fairly simple to arrange and quite suitable for towns as well.

The main challenge is finding the tellers and helping them prepare their stories. Instead of working with each person one-on-one, Yaconelli gets the group together and they serve as a preliminary audience and as mutual aid. James di Properzio, who has twice told stories at The Hearth and watches podcasts from The Moth, agrees preparation provides for better results and enjoys the feeling of close listening by (and empathy from) the audience.

Just as The Hearth itself is a social invention, our

community has social inventions that deal with bullying, which, as mentioned earlier, was the subject of a recent evening of storytelling. In order to help kids relate in ways beyond simply gathering in cliques and picking on others, Yaconelli has drawn upon several local programs that go into schools (The Edge, Mediation Works) or mentor individual young people (Boys to Men, The Rose Circle).

These social inventions didn't exist until somebody asked "Why don't we...?" and started them. Some of the programs get grants, but all depend on volunteers. And any of them could be started in other towns as stand-alone projects through service clubs, churches, or other religious groups.

# CHAPTER 3

# Baby Bonding for Dads

*Here's a conversation from my TV show about people doing something admirable, the first of nine such chapters in this book. Raised in Buffalo, New York, James di Properzio attended St. John's College and did graduate work in philosophy at Emory University. More relevant to the subject of this interview, he became a father in 1999 and now has four children. With his wife, Jennifer Margulis, he has written a book called* The Baby Bonding Book for Dads.

**CKC: Why do we need a book about bonding for dads?**

**JdiP:** When I first became a father, as far as I could tell, there wasn't such a book. The idea of fathers stepping up to become more engaged was pretty new. When I would take our first child to a play group I would always be the only dad. And people would comment, very positively, "Look, there's a dad going to the post office with his six-week-old baby." I wanted to be more engaged than my parents' generation, but I didn't really know how. So much of parenting is through modeling—usually more than we want. We all have things our parents did or said and we say, "I'm never going to do *that* to my kids." Then you grow up and have kids and find the same things coming out of your mouth.

**CKC: What modeling did you have as a child?**

**JdiP:** My dad was really great when I was very small, but he worked two jobs, so he was gone twelve to sixteen hours a day. But when he was there, first thing in the morning and late in the evening, he was really engaged. It was an exciting time for me when he would come home. I would look forward to it. It really was a bonding time.

**CKC: There's a lovely story in the book about your being perched in the bathroom.**

**JdiP:** He would get up in the dark, and I'd be awake. He'd pick me up and perch me up in the bathroom while he was shaving and brushing his teeth, then he'd take me into the kitchen and sit me on the counter. We'd eat some Raisin Bran together. That formed the bonding memories that are still strong. When my eldest child was from one-and-a-half to two, and my second daughter was just a baby, I was working as an editor at Merriam-Webster and had to commute about two hours round trip. So I was gone for a long time, basically from when they woke up until the time they went to sleep. I would see them just for a short time on either side of my day at work. While my wife and the baby would sleep in, my eldest daughter Hesperus would wake up and I'd take her with me as I got ready—just as my dad had done. One of the cute things she did, which I don't recall ever doing, was she would want to shave me.

**CKC: I knew a young man who got married but wanted children "someday"—just not quite yet—so he was very reluctant to be a father until his first child was born (whom he called Jack after one of his heroes, Jack Kerouac). Then he went totally to the other side—I'd never seen a more devoted father.  What have you seen, among young fathers?**

**JdiP:** There was a transformation, certainly for me. I was an only child. I used to say that I guess I wanted *a* child, someday.

**CKC: You guessed? "Someday?"**

**JdiP:** If I were really pressed on it, I would have said, yes, definitely, I want one. Maybe even one of each gender.

**CKC: And you have now?**

**JdiP:** Four. Both genders. I think it was when my wife was expecting and I wondered, "What is my role going to be here? What is it going to be like for me to have a child?" that I realized I didn't want to be a second-class parent. You know, the parent who steps back and is present for a few minutes here and there, and isn't really engaged.

**CKC: Like a Victorian father, appearing late in the afternoon for an audience.**

**JdiP:** Popping into the nursery (same for a Victorian mother!). I knew I wanted to be more engaged. I wanted to have a substantial relationship with my kids.

**CKC: So what did you do?**

**JdiP:** My wife was reading all kinds of books when she was pregnant, and she would pass them over to me sometimes and I would read a section, but I wasn't really motivated to plow through all these "gee-whiz, you're pregnant" books— which were not really aimed at me anyway. I remember walking into a bookstore in Atlanta where we lived at the time and looking for something for fathers, and not finding it. Certainly I didn't see anyone trying to map out the transition from "where does my generation go, having been raised with positive experiences but wanting to be more engaged, wanting to be an equal parent."

I think we're hearing the echo of the drive for women's equality, one generation later, because now it's those women whose children are having kids and their husbands are saying, "I want to be an equal parent." It's more automatic for women. Of course some women have difficulties bonding, but when you have a baby growing inside you …

**CKC: It's a clue.**

**JdiP:** She's already having a bonding experience with the baby. It's not even born yet. But the father is going to have to *develop* a relationship. It's entirely up to you. You can do as little or as much of it as you want.

**CKC: A big theme of your book is "You have to have skin in the game."**

**JdiP:** Yes, it's something that's underrated in our culture in the way we practice our parenting. The baby comes out. They're still pretty floppy. They're not sitting up by themselves. People get those carriers, with a built-in curve, and a handle over the top, like a basket. Parents can carry the child around, put them down: they sit, as long as they're content. But all that time they're not being touched or directly stimulated. They can look around, but they're not getting that direct contact. In contrast, look at a so-called primitive society (primitive in a positive sense) where they're doing something closer to the way we evolved to treat our children. They're always holding them. You can't put them down on the ground. Remember how tactile you are when you're a small child? How good it feels to be held, on a lap? They need a lot of that. With a young baby, who is not talking or even focusing on your face yet, it's all tactile.

**CKC: The biggest challenge for young fathers is what?**

**JdiP:** The *only* challenge is entirely inside themselves: making the transition. In some sense the target audience for *Baby Bonding for Dads* is me. I mean, your wife is going to act more confident about how to take care of the child. Every time she does something confidently, and you're a little bit not so sure, you're going to be a half-step back or a half-second late, and she's going to do it. You have to be much more active. You have to watch yourself in order not to take a step back or go out to do something else, "let" her do what she will quietly and often uncomplainingly do, leaving you once removed. It's so hard to put yourself into a new role like that when you don't have a model.

**CKC: So it's easy to say, "that's women's work, it comes naturally to them?"**

**JdiP:** Sure, one can say that, but it's not even a matter of saying it. It's a matter of how much you've internalized that. I had never held a baby when our first was born; I had no idea what it would be like. I was surprised by how light she was. Changing the baby is not a big deal. People shy away from it. You'll see a lot of fathers, especially the fathers of fathers today, like my own dad, who would never touch a diaper. When Mohammed Ali's wife was expecting their first child, there was a press conference and one of the journalists, to be funny, asked the champ whether he was going to change diapers, and he said angrily that was women's work. Years later his wife revealed that when they took the baby home, she expected to change all the diapers, but he was always very eager to take the baby, to give her some space, and she noticed that the diapers got changed. He had taught himself how to do it.

# CHAPTER 4

# A Center for Artists

*Ashland, Oregon is known as an art center, with more galleries than usual for a town of 20,000. Each month, on the first Friday, even in winter, crowds walk among the galleries. Meanwhile artists often work at home, or in studios that are not always warm in the winter or cool in the summer. Or affordable, or where there are other artists. What if you could put together a center that combined good studios, a shop for supplies, a gathering place for artists and patrons, and a classroom? This was the vision of the Ashland Art Center and its founding director, Denise Baxter.*

**CKC: Denise, start with a brief description of the Art Center.**

**DB:** It's downtown, about 9000 square feet on three floors, and we occupy every inch. A former furniture store, the building required only some divider walls to create studios for artists, and a skylight in the atrium.

**CKC: What is going on in all that space?**

**DB:** After you walk up a grand staircase there is a lounge, and then in either direction you encounter studios with artists working right there, making beautiful paintings and other objects. We have twenty local artists, and the studios are separated by partitions only about five feet high. The space has got a beautiful vibe. The artists are interacting with each other and with the public, seven days a week from 10 a.m. to 6 p.m.

**CKC: Members of the public can come in while the artists are working?**

**DB:** Absolutely, artists who have chosen to come into one of our studios understand that from the beginning. Part of their role is to allow community access, to be open, and to enjoy the interaction. That elevates the understanding of art, the appreciation of art, and also increases their sales. Part of what the Art Center does is help the artists become better business people, and that in turn creates a better business climate in the town.

**CKC: You have a background running a gallery, and are also a painter.**

**DB:** I think of myself as a painter first. Although I am not painting now, that's what I am best at, but it was so natural for me that I took it for granted. For ten years I tried to become a businessperson. I felt painting is so easy. I got a couple of masters degrees in business management and worked super hard—running a business never felt easy, it was a real challenge for me. Being able to couple my passion for art with skills that I cultivated in business made it possible for us to get where we are today with the Art Center.

**CKC: One day I saw you painting a pathway design on the floor.**

**DB:** People started feeling sorry for me because I was always in there, sometimes doing manual labor. But that's what it took at that stage, when we were doing renovations—sweat equity.

**CKC: You have talked about the second floor. What is on the ground floor?**

**DB:** From the main entrance you walk into a gallery. Of 200 artist members we have a committee to select the ones we will represent in the gallery—currently we have more than thirty, many who take turns working behind the cash register. After a twelve-month period, we evaluate the sales of our gallery artists, and some will be brought back in for the next year. Profits from the gallery help support the Art Center, and it's been a positive experience for the artists because we carefully evaluate their work and try to feature what sells.

Then we have a rotating gallery for artist members; a satellite of a well-known local art store; a commercial photographer who does artists' profiles; a graphic designer corner; and at the back a check-in counter for a community art space that also includes a huge classroom.

Downstairs, on the lower floor, we have studios and kilns for ceramics, plus studios for printmaking and individual artists.

**CKC: What pays for all this—surely not just sales in the gallery?**

**DB:** No. The ability to generate revenue streams from all directions was a big part of creating the business plan at the start, so we've really needed to think outside the box. We have leases for the artists' studios, membership fees from other artists, community memberships, classes, and foundations—although during the economic contraction foundations in general had less to give. In order to give to a new organization, a foundation has to cut back on what it gives to existing beneficiaries. I have a lot of empathy for what the trustees must go through.

**CKC: In my sordid past I was, among other things, a foundation director. We loved to give to people who did not know that something could not be done, who went ahead and just did it. For this you would be a prime candidate.**

**DB:** Under normal circumstances we probably would've been able to get quite a bit of foundation funding, but in the wake of 2008 it's been a difficult period for the foundations. My business plan, though we need and expect grants, is inspired by the for-profit sector, so when I was creating our structure I initially didn't even think about grants. Now I am realizing that grants will help us be even better.

**CKC: In many institutes and centers such as yours there is a combination of artists or researchers and people who know business, and without the latter it just doesn't happen.**

**DB:** I had to work extra hard at the business side of it and had the good fortune to be surrounded by really good people. For the board of directors, I pulled from all sectors. They are all leaders in our community, such as a man from the construction industry, an architect, an interior designer, and many others.

**CKC: The space you described is rather different from a furniture store. What was involved in creating it?**

**DB:** Members of the board donated their professional services. Of course we also had to raise money, which was a big challenge. We had to build bathrooms for the public, to code. We had to acquire brand new fixtures throughout, flooring, and studio partitions. We received a lot of donations of materials, such as the sheet rock and bathroom fixtures.

**CKC: Let's go back to the second floor for a moment. Are these studios galleries, or working spaces for the artists?**

**DB:** Really a combination of the two. We look closely at applicants and we have a lot of photographers right now, perhaps four out of the twenty upstairs spaces. When people from the community visit, we want them to see a good selection of media.

**CKC: I've been told that galleries here depend heavily on summer visitors. How is the street traffic in other seasons?**

**DB:** It's not as scary as when I was a gallery owner. There is still a flow because artists are here working.

I hope because we have the community room available, that will help bring people in. They can come in, purchase a $3 hunk of clay, and take their child down to the ceramic room, which is nice and warm, and make art.

**CKC: Do you have a program with the schools at all?**

**DB:** We do, and I have so many dreams. For example, I'd like to find a room where we can work with the kids after school once a week. Meanwhile, we have started a mentorship program with the Wilderness Charter School and are pairing twelve of their juniors and seniors with artists.

It's a big issue for me: I remember being in second grade and not being able to read. My brain was constantly going. I couldn't focus, would sit there with my book and turn the page when the rest of the class did. It was self-defeating and difficult. But I had wonderful support with my art and believe that I was able to fall back on the realization that I am an artist. I'm not good at reading, or great at math, but I can make art. That has carried through with me my entire life. All the way to graduate school when I had to work twice as hard in order to get my "B." There are kids out there like that who need support, especially with cuts in the school budget.

**CKC: What do these mentors do?**

**DB:** The mentors have the choice of using the Art Center room or the studios in their homes. And the students will learn to make a specific kind of art. One student who fell in love with some art that she saw at the center came to me and said, "Can I work with this artist?" So I called the artist and said the student wanted to work with her, and she said, "Great!" Another student was just going crazy over some sculpture she saw, and asked whether she could work with that artist. We are a resource for the community, with over 200 artists. Every single artist has a website page, and they're often in the center.

**CKC: You have many artists who do not have studios in the building, but who have a page on the website.**

**DB:** Yes. To be an Art Center artist, you pay $50 per year, and for that you get a website page, listings, you can even have a video—we take care of all that for you. You are also automatically in the database, you may participate in the development workshops at cost, and have the possibility of a free show.

**CKC: A show in the rotating gallery?**

**DB:** Yes, and in the main gallery—we look at every artist's work—and also in one of our seven outside exhibiting venues, such as the hospital, Starbucks, another coffeehouse, the Palace Café, a real estate office. They all look to our website for art to exhibit.

## CHAPTER 5

# Abundance Gifting

Somewhere in the holiday season, between shoppers breaking down Walmart doors on Black Friday and the wise men showing up with gifts for the baby Jesus, my town holds an event known as the Abundance Swap.

The name could be somewhat misleading, because participants do not trade items one-on-one and bargain in the hope of getting a good deal. Instead, they are asked to donate several things they'd be happy to receive as gifts, and after an introduction, to take three of anything they like in the room, with no trading at all. It's an introduction to the gift culture, as if the whole community were one big family.

Started eleven years ago as a social invention, the abundance event now attracts hundreds of people, filling the old armory, a big downtown venue. They come bearing gifts, receive nametags, and socialize while awaiting the first of three rounds determined by the color of one's tag.

Asked one year why I volunteered at the swap, I replied, as a joke, that I was hoping to get a big TV. A few moments later a woman arrived and asked for help bringing in an item. In her station wagon, as you will guess, was a TV. Of course it went to someone else, not a staff member, but it showed the generosity that the event hopes to elicit.

What's the serious answer about why I, and many others, volunteer? Because it's fun to help a little as people give stuff.

At worst, the items are what you'd find at a garage sale;

at best, what you'd hope to unwrap as a gift. No money changes hands. With rare exceptions, a participant's three items go to one set of people, while the giver takes items donated by other people.

When they are not circulating to find something they want, participants stay with the gifts they are donating. This enables them to converse with people attracted to what they brought, and to tell a little about the history of the items.

Does anybody try to "game the system," as if he or she were a Wall Street banker? Of course, but most people are delighted by what Bill Maher would call a "new rule"—give freely, then take what you want.

The event came out of a men's group called "The Relentless Optimists," which sought to encourage social inventions and was the particular brainchild of Jeff Golden, then a local radio host. It's now real enough to have its own website, so you can check out the details by simply googling "Abundance Swap."

As a member of the staff I have had the opportunity to ask many participants why they come. For some it's the atmosphere, so different from Black Friday and what has become the pervasive consumerism of December. For others, it's a way to get nice stuff they can't afford for the kids' Christmas gifts.

It's a time when folks are experimenting with many alternatives to consumerism. In the case of the magazine *Adbusters* (which had a hand in inspiring Occupy Wall Street), its contribution is an analysis of a culture that spends millions on inculcating the messages "you are what you can get" and "he who dies with the most toys wins."

While some people urge a gift-less holiday season, many in our community share the abundance they have in a form that allows the special joy of giving. A current theoretician of the gift culture, Charles Eisenstein, encourages us to transition to a more connected, ecological, and sustainable way of being in his book *Sacred Economics*.

Although the Abundance Swap is currently held in a privately owned venue, it has also taken place in a city building and in a church hall. Anybody can start an abundance gifting event by obtaining use of a space with some tables, rounding up a few volunteers, and, in advance, a helpful local reporter or two.

# CHAPTER 6

# Learning for Elders

*Our subject for this show is lifelong learning, which in Ashland takes the form of a program called OLLI (Osher Lifelong Learning Institute), and our guest is Anne Bellegia, a volunteer involved with community relations.*

**CKC: Welcome, Anne. What does OLLI do?**

**AB:** It started in Ashland in 1993, so it's more than two decades old. It's a program for older adults. We have about 1500 members and provide a lot of different opportunities for learning. Our members are eligible to choose from eighty to one hundred classes every quarter that are all over the map in terms of topics and formats, including discussion groups, lectures, and outdoor activities.

**CKC: How do you get to be a member?**

**AB:** By paying the annual membership fee, which is currently $125. The fee covers all three quarters of the academic year, with the opportunity to take as many courses as you can get scheduled. Some people, like my husband, take six courses per quarter.

**CKC: That's more than many undergraduates take.**

**AB:** Yes, but there are no tests, grades, or prerequisites, so it's a lot more fun. And there's nobody saying you must take a certain topic, at a certain time.

**CKC: When I attended my first OLLI course it took me several minutes to realize that I wouldn't be graded.**

**AB:** You can just explore, have fun, and ask questions. You don't have to feel they are dumb questions, because the students are from all kinds of backgrounds: while some have a depth of knowledge on the topic, others take courses that are 180 degrees in a different direction from what they might have worked at or studied as an undergraduate.

**CKC: Are the teachers mainly people who have taught as their career?**

**AB:** We get a variety of teachers because we live in a very rich community of retired people, including professors from institutions all over the country. Then we also get people who have taught in elementary, middle, and high schools. We also have people like myself who have never taught anything, for whom teaching is an exciting challenge—figuring out what you want to say and how you can communicate it.

**CKC: It sounds as if you have a national collection of potential teachers.**

**AB:** Actually, from many places in the world. We are fortunate in having a rich pool of potential instructors, including the hidden gems of people who have never taught but are willing to. Some teachers will select a topic in which they have a great depth—for example, we have someone teaching on healthcare reform who was a health care administrator. We also have people veering off in other directions. We've had the inventor of the world's first microprocessor teaching a cooking class, an expert in distribution management teaching military history. This gives the instructors a chance to broaden themselves. And the ones who are teaching in an area where they have a lot of depth may find out that their field has evolved. We have a cell biologist teaching a course on the human microbiome (for example, genes of organisms in the intestines), which required doing a little homework.

**CKC: I imagine OLLI is attractive to potential teachers because of the reasons you have given and also because the learners are so enthusiastic. They are not coming because of a requirement, they *want* to be in the class.**

**AB:** People who have taught in the past say, "I'm so glad nobody is raising their hand and asking, 'Is this going to be on the test?'" The student enthusiasm is incredible, and the questions asked often make the instructors think.

**CKC: The cliché in America about elders is we're interested only in things like golf and shuffleboard, but in fact you have this large audience.**

**AB:** It surprises younger people sometimes to find out how complex their elders are. If they first look at someone who is older they may think, "what a sweet, grandmotherly person," or maybe an elder is invisible to a younger person. That's a complaint we hear. One of the gems for me in interacting with other OLLI students is finding out the incredible background and stories they have—background you might not think exists to just look at them. We have public lectures as well as classes. One of the lecturers discussed her experience sailing around the world as a young woman pre-GPS (global positioning system). It was scary stuff for me to think about. I find that all the time, the surprise factor.

**CKC: I gather the "O" in OLLI stands for Osher. What is that?**

**AB:** When OLLI was first formed, it was called SOLAR— Southern Oregon Learning and Retirement. At some point we realized that our facilities were aging, our equipment was kind of not too modern, so we decided to look for a grant.

It turned out that Bernard Osher had formed a foundation that supports lifelong learning for older adults. In fact, there are almost 120 programs on university campuses around the country that are benefiting from his generosity. When we accepted the grant and endowment from the Osher Foundation, we became part of this network.[6]

**CKC: How far flung is the network?**

**AB:** From Maine to Hawaii. We're starting to get people in the Rogue Valley who have selected this area in which to retire because they are aware we have an OLLI program.

**CKC: Another attraction for our area, like the Shakespeare festival or the hiking trails?**

AB: Exactly. We're fortunate here in having such a diversity of attractions, both cultural and outdoor. Staying stimulated is a big issue for older adults. We're no longer relying on our work lives to keep us vibrant and engaged.

**CKC: Does OLLI run mainly on volunteers who are the teachers?**

**AB:** We do have paid staff, but their role is mainly to support the logistics of the organization, make sure we have a roof over our heads, equipment that's working. The members are tasked with creating the program content, teaching courses, hosting classes, providing the communication vehicles for members, running social events, raising money for projects that we want to underwrite. I guess I'm a cheerleader for how important volunteerism is for the individual. Of course it benefits the organization, but individuals who volunteer have better cognition, health, longevity. They're getting these little squirts of oxytocin every time they give in some way.

**CKC: Could that be a motto for OLLI, "squirts of oxytocin"?**

**AB:** One of our mottos is "connect with other curious minds." I think curiosity is definitely the elixir of youth—as long as you're learning and evolving, life is just so much more fun.

**CKC: What are some of the new directions for OLLI?**

**AB:** There are many learning formats that we're exploring. We've talked about travel opportunities. We've talked about courses that are more hands-on. We have opportunities for more inter-generational contact with Southern Oregon University (SOU). We have contacts with Science Works; with COHO ("Choosing Options, Honoring Options") an organization focused on preparations for end of life; with Ashland At Home, helping neighbors to age in place. So far we've been in the taking role and have benefited from facilities, guidance, and management of our endowment, but we have a lot of young people on the campus who could benefit from the knowledge and experience of our members.

**CKC: The Rose Circle (see Chapter 12) and the Boys to Men Program (Chapter 13) have stressed the importance of mentoring.**

**AB:** We have started a program on mentoring with the SOU Honors College, but we could be doing more. Young people are graduating without the benefits of a good job market, which I enjoyed when I got out of college. How do you apply for a job? It's an abstraction until you have to do it. There are also opportunities for us to model how learning is valuable intrinsically. It's not necessarily just to get a job it's important for our brains.

**CKC: Young students who feel compelled to go to a class because it's a requirement can find at OLLI people who are fifty or older who want to be in a class?**

**AB:** And Oregonians who are sixty-five and older can audit classes at SOU, with the instructor's permission, which some OLLI members have done. Some undergraduates say, "You don't even have to be here," or "Why are you here?" OLLI auditors can also listen to some of the undergraduate drama and help them think about organizing their lives in different ways.

# CHAPTER 7

# New Tribes

*Another conversation from my RVTV program,* Like, Wow!

**CKC: Our guests today are the co-authors of a book called *We Need Each Other*, Bill Kauth and Zoe Alowan. I'm going to let them introduce each other.**

**ZA:** Bill is one of my favorite social visionaries. About twenty-eight years ago he had a vision to create a training program for men and he cofounded The Mankind Project, which is all over the world now with about 50,000 members. He also did something called the Inner King Training for Men, and then for ten years traveled around the world doing something called "The Warrior Monk" for men and women. And when we met, we began doing this work of building a community of men and women together. He is extremely persevering.

**CKC: A good quality. Bill?**

**BK:** Zoe and I met at Burning Man back in 2005 and I recognized right away this is one extraordinarily splendid human being, so I courted her and we married in 2008. One of the beautiful things about Zoe is she really loves community. As she suggested I've been building men's communities for most of my adult life. The time is right to build community for men and women together. Zoe brings to the party the fact that she's an amazing artist in so many areas. She does painting and sculpture; my favorites are her singing, dancing, and storytelling. As a team, we work together well.

**CKC: You've written a book together,** *We Need Each Other.* **Does our culture teach something different?**

**ZA:** This culture monetizes everything. Money is king. All the things that used to be near and dear to people—like child care and taking care of the elderly—can now be bought for a price. People have become so individuated in this culture, so separate, that they have forgotten a lot of the qualities of reciprocity, of give and take, and the fact that we really *do* need each other.

**CKC: When you talk about tribe, what in particular do you mean?**

**BK:** We're the loneliest culture in the history of the world. (Also the wealthiest.) Everything in our culture pulls us apart from each other. It's been destroying community for half a century. Our huge task is to re-communalize, to re-tribalize the entire culture. We stopped using the word community a little while back because it's too big: there's the national community, the local community, etc. We've chosen the word "tribe" because it reflects something we once had when people lived in deeply bonded, loving, small groups. We have it in us. We say: "You can take a person out of the tribe, but you can't take 'tribe' out of a person." We can't actually go back to the old way, because we've evolved so much psychologically and spiritually, so we have to create what we're calling "new tribe." New tribe is for those of us who have evolved in such a way that we need a new way of meeting each other and being together.

**CKC: It sounds in some ways like the 1970s intentional community. Is what you're talking about, residential?**

**BK:** We're not talking about living together. We're talking about everybody having their own home or place to live. We want to learn how to get on the same page, to help people find others with the same values, the same intentions. We make commitments to each other. We become a tribe.

**ZA:** In this time, in this town, we ask people, "Are you committed to staying in this bio-region?" That's extremely challenging for people because many want to be free to go to Nova Scotia if that's where spirit is calling them, or that's where the best job is. To New York, or Tahiti, or Santa Fe. The world is now small, you can move around. But commitment to a bio-region, as Gary Snyder was the first to tell me, is essential. It's a commitment to place. We were just in Australia doing seminars and we got a chance to spend time with aboriginal elders, including a woman in her seventies. Among aborigines, instead of, "I think, therefore I am," they would say: "I am located, therefore I am." They describe where they live, the tribe and clan names. In our culture how identified are we with the Rogue River, with the Cuyahoga, the Tuolumne?

**CKC: So you're asking people not to live in the same structure, but to stay in the same bioregion?**

**BK:** If they don't make a commitment to stay in the same place, they will never become a bonded tribe such as we are building.

**ZA:** We're not opposed to people living in the same building, but how many times over the past thirty years have we experienced people saying "We're going to get a piece of land, we're all going to live there, and it's all going to work out," but they haven't done their conflict resolution or developed gender-safety skills? So we thought it important to live in your own home while building relationships with each other.

**CKC: I know you were both involved in a workshop that emphasized nonsexual intimacy. What did that allow you to do?**

**ZA:** That was one of the beginning points of our connection, when we met at Burning Man. I had gone through a training that involved a period of time when you worked, in a group only with women, on your father wound; a period when you worked on your mother wound. Then we met with men in the larger group. Once you graduated from that program you could do a seven-day training with men and women together, twenty-four hours a day, called "clearing the air," which was between men and women who had done the deep personal work. (That's where I first heard about the New Warrior training—the men who went through the training that Bill helped to start were so much more emotionally literate.) In the training we did, we had to sign an agreement that we would never be sexual with anyone else in that group. This agreement created a tremendous amount of safety. Then Bill went and did the training later. Luckily we weren't in the same group.

**BK:** My learning curve was enormous, being with women in this unique, safe way. And that led to a community that extended about 500 miles. We'd get together once a quarter. It was beautiful, intimate, wonderful, but Zoe and I wanted to have such a community right here in Ashland. So we started out about five years ago, studying the scant literature. We realized we'd have to create it ourselves. We made a lot of mistakes. Things we didn't know. Things you can only discover by getting in with both feet. A year ago we developed what we call the orientation and initiation, a five-week training in which everyone we invite goes through a learning funnel into the tribe. That involves some pretty deep intimacy work where we learn to trust each other at a deep level; and conflict resolution, of course, and gender safety. We need to get everybody on the same page in terms of being absolutely transparent with each other, so those kinds of secrets don't later emerge that really hurt the community or tribe. We're giving a workshop for people coming in from around the country how to do this precise training so when they bring their friends together they can build a deep, long-term, intimate tribe that lasts a lifetime.

**CKC: Zoe, you mentioned gift community early on, and you have sponsored a workshop with Charles Eisenstein. Does the New Tribes movement come out of his work?**

**ZA:** We were both very drawn to building community, and Bill, around the time he and I met, did something in Ashland called "In My Village." There was quite a turnout, but it dwindled away, as so many things do. In the community in northern California, which would come together quarterly, people would say, "This is my family of choice." We thought, we can do that, and started to find the structures needed and to write them out. As we were engaged in bringing people together for an intentional family, a family of choice, Charles Eisenstein came into our consciousness through his book *The Ascent of Humanity*. We invited him out here several times, then we did a five-day workshop out at Buckhorn Springs. Charles has a brilliant way of speaking about gift culture.

**BK:** The workshop was called "Seeing the Gift Culture." In beautiful, essential detail he taught us how we're moving from the old capitalist paradigm, which has done its job— it's done now—to another way of being, which has to do with being transparent, with gifting each other. It still has reciprocity, but it's not that kind of hard monetization of everything. Once you have a monetary transaction, it's done, and we're strangers again. We're looking for more of an interdependent way of being, and we see it coming as we go into our own hearts to create the kind of tribe in which we really want to live.

**CKC: You're building a particular tribe, too?**

**ZA:** We've been tilling the soil of gift culture. It's about moving from transaction to trust. You can't build a real community, a personal community, without trust. Moving from isolation to connection is a way we're changing. In our first workshop, one of the participants coined the term "gift circles." We created such a circle here in Ashland. We sit together once a month, have a wonderful potluck, then go around the circle with each saying what we need. Other people in the circle will think of ways in which they can meet that need. Similar circles have started around the country. It's huge, for people to ask for what they want.

**BK:** We've chosen people we feel are ready, people we want to be with in our tribe, and we ran the first four through the training, and they became staff or leaders to bring the next six through, so then we had ten committed, plus Zoe and me. And then we did the training with nine more and had a tribe of twenty-one with an expectation of being together for the rest of our lives. (Even though we only ask for a one-year commitment at a time.) I think now we've got the piece that we've been missing for so long.

**CKC: What is that piece you were looking for?**

**ZA:** I see you as a gift. I see myself as a gift. That's a big step. How can we support each other to give our gifts in the world? It's not the same as, "How can I get something for free?" Or bartering, where if you give me that, I'll give you this. It's more about having a deep conversation and investigation of how we can live life on this earth as the gift that we came here to give.

**CLC: So what do people have more hesitation about, asking for something or offering it?**

**ZA:** Asking terrifies people—it's very much a stretch. We've had people say, "I could never ask for what you asked for. I don't feel worthy."

**BK:** Worthy enough to receive.

**ZA:** Asking is the hard part. For example, we had people meeting at our house all the time. The house has white carpets. They got a little affected by all this traffic. I asked for help with cleaning the carpets. I had a back problem. It took me about a year to receive that gift. I thought, "First I'm going to have to clean up all my messy corners." Finally I understood that I had to let them *see* my messy corners.

**CKC: It sounds as if you are applying that principle very widely, letting people see the messy corners of more than the house.**

**BK:** We create enough safety so people get to know each other pretty deeply. And from that place comes a kind of trust, which creates something that I call "liminal space," meaning "threshold," an incredibly deep, trusting presence. We've all experienced this in brief seminars, but I wanted to feel that trust every week in our tribe, and I set that goal, even wrote it down, and we have it now. Every week when we get together we kind of go to heaven together. We find that place very quickly. We touch, make a little physical contact, do some music, we're right there, every single week: exquisite. That's what I want for everybody. We can do this. We have done this. We can teach others how to do it.

**CKC: If this gets really big, there would be many tribes, and in each tribe there would be many "families"?**

**BK:** I imagine Ashland having 100 tribes. True, some folks are so not ready for it, so afraid of getting too close. Not in this lifetime are they going to be in the kind of tribe we're talking about. But there are also a couple of hundred million on the planet who are ready.

**CKC: Would the tribes interact in some way? Some of the founding people of this country were very impressed by the Iroquois Confederacy, a set of five tribes. They had wonderful practices, such as the provision that going to war had to be approved by the grandmothers.**

**BK:** I like that idea. Can you imagine every quarter the tribes having some sort of congregation, sharing best practices, what's working in their tribe?

# Leadership

## CHAPTER 8

# Make Me Do It

*Recently a friend who is an older person, but claims not to be especially wise—"just a guy"—had the opportunity to confer with someone he considers to be a "real" elder. My friend prepared his questions carefully, and also his technology. When they met, he used his smartphone to capture the audio. This is how it went down:*

**Guy: How do we find transformational leaders?**

**Elder** (in a kindly tone): Wrong question, lad.

**Guy: You don't think the U.S. political situation is desperately in need of change?**

**Elder:** Totally desperate, but your initial query is blinded by an assumption.

**Guy (evasively): My friends and I just want to find a transformational leader we can believe in.**

**Elder:** That's the problem. You're easily flattered. Are you the people you've been waiting for? A candidate emerges from the meritocracy and talks pretty, but meanwhile accepts hefty funds from the financial elite.

**Guy: Well, we tried.**

**Elder:** And he turned out, on some big issues, to accept policies that were not sharply different from his predecessor.

**Guy:** I thought he and his allies might fight for Single Payer health insurance (such as the rest of the developed world has). I hoped he would effectively regulate Wall Street and get out of Iraq (rather than rebranding the troops there as "trainers").

**Elder:** Whoa, young fella, you've got two problems. Your leader may not be who you hoped that he was, but even if he were, do you expect anyone to transform the system by himself?

**Guy: He's not alone. I keep fairly well informed. And I can't tell you how many Internet petitions I've signed.**

**Elder:** Paul Rogat Loeb, author of *Soul of a Citizen,* calls this the "seduction of clicking." Do you think the system is afraid of Internet warriors?

**Guy (explaining it's somebody else's fault): Everything seems to get lost in the swamp of Congress.**

**Elder:** Pity your poor legislators who have to spend most spare moments "dialing for dollars." Can you be astonished that they feel gratitude to executives, lobbyists, front groups, and even now to corporations that are allowed to give big chunks of money? This practice is perfectly legal, it's not prosecutable as bribery. The money is to support a campaign, not to buy a specific vote.

**Guy (who sees where the elder is going): Well, let me say I haven't supported campaigns financed solely by public funds: why should we citizens pay for those crooks to lie to us?**

**Elder:** I understand. But is this frugality or false economy? Don't you end up paying many times as much when big money interests get laws and regulations they want?

**Guy: So you regard the whole system as corrupt?**

**Elder:** Not the whole system; your political system has many revolutionary and admirable components. But as long as you allow big money to distort your elections and the legislative process, Congress will block any change that would challenge big money. It's really quite simple.

**Guy (hopefully): We're about to elect a new House and a third of the Senate.**

**Elder:** I know, but how many legislators of either party will stand up for ordinary citizens? They say they will, but "he who pays the piper calls the tune."

**Guy: But ultimately doesn't the majority rule?**

**Elder:** According to surveys, big groups of voters have wanted Single Payer health insurance, strict regulation of big banks, background checks for gun buyers, an end to the wars in Iraq and Afghanistan. Do you see any of this happening, except in the form of spin?

**Guy: Okay, so what do you want?**

**Elder:** I want nonviolent but widespread, persistent, simple demands for programs that benefit the whole community, not just the richest 1% or 5% or 10%.

**Guy: Isn't this exactly what we hoped that a transformational leader would do?**

**Elder:** During The Great Depression FDR said to a movement leader—with whom he agreed—"Make me do it." As long as you sit back and depend on a leader, you're going to be disappointed, even when the leader could be transformational.

**Guy: I thought it was pretty good that so many of us got to the polls.**

**Elder:** Yes, it was a good start, but leaders respond to pressure, to an aroused public. The first serious environmental laws were passed in Nixon's time; voting rights laws in the presidency of a southerner, of LBJ. In each case the leaders were pushed by a movement.

**Guy: So what do we put on the bumper sticker?**

**Elder:** As they used to say in the citizen diplomacy movement, back during the Cold War: "When the people lead, the leaders will follow."

CHAPTER 9

# The Power of Compassion

The admirable Canada of the Vietnam War era is back. Fresh from showing up his ruling conservative opponents in the Canadian election, and from appointing a gender-balanced cabinet, new Prime Minister Justin Trudeau has shown up the entire GOP presidential field with regard to the Syrian refugees. In contrast to fear mongering and bullying, Trudeau personally welcomed the first planeload of "new Canadians" from Syria, and made sure they had social insurance numbers, health cards, and winter coats.

Of course, this arrival of refugees was not only an opportunity to draw a maximum contrast with fear-driven neighbors to the south (not for the first time), but also an act of compassion. "This is a wonderful night when we get to show not just a plane load of new Canadians what Canada's all about," said Trudeau, "we get to show the world how to open our hearts and welcome in people who are fleeing extraordinarily difficult situations."

How to open our hearts, how to access that part of ourselves that wants to help people, to listen to them, to imagine their life experience, their viewpoint. While empathy is not a panacea, and the practice can be done to manipulate, it can also enlarge our comfort zones, help us learn about the world, even reach out to enemies.

The great commencement speech delivered at American University in 1963 by President Kennedy is an excellent example. Seeking peace in the Cold War, he demonstrated empathy when he described how the Second World War was experienced by the U.S.S.R.—then a wartime ally, but at the time of the speech our Cold War enemy. Specifically, JFK asked his audience to imagine what would have happened if the Nazis had invaded the U.S. as they did the U.S.S.R. when he said:

"... No nation in the history of battle ever suffered more than the Soviet Union in the Second World War. At least twenty million lost their lives. Countless millions of homes and farms were burned or sacked. A third of the nation's territory, including two-thirds of its industrial base, was turned into a wasteland—a loss equivalent to the destruction of this country east of Chicago."

When I visited Moscow as a "citizen diplomat" in 1986, right after the Reykjavik Summit between Gorbachev and Reagan, people were still referring to JFK's speech, which had been delivered twenty-three years earlier.[7]

For me, the most recent occasion for trying to understand an experience foreign to me was writing a book called *Gift of Darkness: Growing Up in Occupied Amsterdam*.[8] It's the bio of a Jewish boy, Robbert Van Santen who (unlike his schoolmate, Anne Frank) managed to survive the Nazis, and whom I met in California half a century later. (*Gift of Darkness is* the first volume in The Gratitude Trilogy, of which *Better Ways to Live* is the third.)

Van Santen and I were worlds apart. He was born in Europe; I, in the U.S. His family was Jewish; mine, Lutheran. Because of the war, his last schooling had been in the seventh grade; I'd attended an Ivy League college. He had made his living as a seller of electrical goods; I, as a writer and coach to authors. As a follower of Rudolph Steiner (founder of the Waldorf Schools), he had a spiritual life; when we met

I was searching, at best.

Moreover, he suggested at the start of our project that he'd provide the facts, to which I'd somehow add "the feelings." I knew this wouldn't work, but was not then alert to the aftermath of trauma. With admirable courage he dove into the memories of his teenage years. On my part the situation was a repeated challenge to empathy, especially because I intended to piece together thousands of fragments into a vivid, present-tense account. (The gratitude that I felt toward him was for being willing to revisit what had been a traumatic time.)

After witnessing the trial in Jerusalem of Adolf Eichmann, a man who served Hitler by delivering people to be murdered, Hannah Arendt was struck by the Nazi bureaucrat's inability "to think from the standpoint of somebody else." Clearly referring to his lack of empathy, Arendt declared that "no communication was possible with him, not because he lied, but because he was surrounded by the most reliable of all safeguards against the words and presence of others, and hence against reality as such." What was this "safeguard," as Arendt ironically calls it? It was Eichmann's inability to experience the world from any standpoint other than his own bureaucratic rules.

As Paul Bloom of Yale points out, empathy can mislead well-intentioned people: we might care more about a single child trapped in a well than about widespread routine suffering about which we remain uninformed or in denial. However, without the skill of empathy a person remains trapped within his or her own viewpoint, unable to understand or even notice the feelings of anybody else.

At least since Gautama Buddha, it's been no secret that while developing a self and a comfort zone in which one can accomplish the tasks of a life, the challenge is to become sensitive and helpful to other selves (to learn the practice of compassion) and then to see the illusory nature of *all* selves. (The second volume in The Gratitude Trilogy is called *Enlarging Our Comfort Zones,* with examples drawn from a decade of my own life, including remarkable people I met and, in some cases, worked with.)

In terms not of ethics but of openness to discovery, many of the main scientific realizations have come as a result of decentering. Until Galileo, our ancestors assumed that the earth was the center of the universe, around which every other celestial body rotated. Before Freud, the unconscious remained largely out of sight as compared with mentation ("I think, therefore I am"). Until Darwin, we humans stood apart from all other life forms and did not notice the evidence for evolution.

In evolutionary terms, if our ancestors survived in part by cooperating with others, and if humans like to be heard, the skill of being able to imagine viewpoints other than our own would have survival value. We may all be self-centered, but to varying extents the ability to understand standpoints and feelings other than our own can be learned. And, on occasion, we can also learn to regard our own feelings and viewpoints as limited, in need of some enlargement.

Roman Krznaric's book, *Empathy,* reminds us of the immense power of imagining other viewpoints, while it also cautions against regarding this practice as a cure-all. In 2009, Jeremy Rifkin declared that empathy could grow until it includes the whole world, and thus could save the world from gross misunderstanding and hostility. While fervently supporting this skill, Krznaric explicitly raises doubts about Rifkin's hope. He is doubtful, too, about the possibility of the Internet fostering deep relationships.

It's possible that nothing has a more dramatic effect than a public figure acting out of compassion rather than fear, as JFK did with regard to the U.S.S.R.; as Trudeau did in welcoming the refugees. Perhaps, in the vision of Adam Hochschild, we could celebrate wise peacemakers as ardently as we have been thanking brave veterans. To the extent we do the former, in a timely way, we might not have to do as much of the latter.

# CHAPTER 10

# Transition Towns

C an we get beyond denial about resource depletion, climate change, and economic troubles if we don't find forms of action open to us?

The genius of the "Transition Town" movement is that it starts with a positive vision, focuses on local scenes, teaches skills, invites people to develop plans, gives them other obviously useful things to do together, and thus provides the added value of intensifying community. You can find all this in its handbook, or online at www.transitionus.org.

Despite the joys of social networking, community only happens when we see people who are *not* on a flatscreen; gathering with them to work, share, argue, and celebrate. This can happen anywhere, but is perhaps easiest in a small town.

Yes, the Transition Movement has limitations; everything does. And it does not directly challenge the corporate and political elites whose actions or inactions determine the context within which localities exist. But the movement does offer a way forward. (As one of my British friends said when I was grumbling, "Let's get on with it, now, shall we?")

Rob Hopkins, who with his colleagues started the Transition Movement, settled in Totnes, a small market town near the south coast of England. And the movement now has affiliates in small towns, and also in the neighborhoods of big cities and in rural areas. While some are still "mulling" over the prospects, others have produced action plans.

The movement does not hide the severity of the challenges from peak oil and climate change. What it offers is a way to consider dire projections, because responses to them suddenly seem possible. These responses have included increases in local food supply, "reskilling," the circulation of local currency, bulk buying of solar panels, building with local materials, teaching about resilience, and the development of Energy Descent Action Plans.

As we find ourselves having to live with less energy, says the movement, we will have to lead our lives more locally, the opposite of globalization. Unable to rely so heavily on imports supplied by faraway factories, mines, and wells—and on industrial agriculture—we will have to use technology that is more appropriate for local food growing, local crafts, and manufacturing.

Though the movement differs in many ways from earlier initiatives, ideas from the 1970s remain in the mix, along with more recent concepts. E.F. Schumacher's *Small is Beautiful: Economics As If People Mattered* was published in 1973. Whatever may be its relations with the Schumacher Society of today, the Transition Movement shares some of its main concerns. And Hopkins is reconceptualizing the transition movement in terms of Christopher Alexander's *A Pattern Language*, published in 1977. Likewise, Hopkins originally taught permaculture, an approach to the natural world described in 1978 by Bill Mollison and David Holmgren.

However, the Transition Movement strives not to "go back to the land," but to increase the resilience of communities. If there is a guiding romance within the movement, it would be less the self-sufficient rural life than the engaged town or neighborhood, rich in human contacts and cooperation.

It's easy, gazing at the upward slope of gross domestic

product, to assume that our society is the best one possible—except for what "growth" will, most people hope, make possible soon. Part of the appeal of the Transition Movement is its quiet doubt about this assumption. Perhaps we can find an even better way of living, even under conditions of "energy descent." (A theme developed further in Chapter 24.)

Among various innovations, Hopkins[9] and his colleagues have rediscovered the attractions of face-to-face democracy. The movement may be local, but as the U.S. Speaker of the House Tip O'Neil once said, "All politics is local." Clearly, if even a small percentage of our many towns mobilize, the central government would begin to take notice. In fact, the British movement attracted a national official as "keynote listener" to one of its conferences.

Judging from afar by watching videos online and by reading reports and comments of participants, the Transition Movement in Totnes attracts many locals who attend celebrations of the work or energy fairs; and at least 75 percent of people in the Totnes area have heard of the movement.

Once people see that it's possible to prepare, at least to some extent, and feel they are not alone, they have a better chance of getting through the stages of adaptation to reality that Carolyn Baker discusses in *Sacred Demise: Walking the Spiritual Path of Industrial Civilization's Collapse.* The nightmare of those who expect hard times is a lack of preparation, psychological as well as physical. If the global peak of oil production drives prices up, affecting economies, and if climate change brings more misallocations of water (drought here, floods there), the shock will be intense for those expecting a return to "growth."

The Transition model of engagement is most effective when people can imagine both severe challenges and a better way of life that doesn't depend on growth. The British Isles are perhaps especially blessed in these ways—when it comes to harsh challenges, Dunkirk, the Blitz, and then the end of empire have not disappeared from memory. Likewise, the English have long had traditions other than consumerism and suburban cocooning. And it was England that produced the "Stern Review," a report on why, in response to climate change, it would cost less to act now than to wait.

It's possible that the U.S., despite already being peppered with transition projects, nonetheless presents a harder case. It's true that in Vietnam, as Leonard Cohen sang with bitter irony, "the good guys lost," and true that the U.S. had a wake-up call on September 11, 2001, but our very being as a nation was not threatened by military invasion or by loss of an entire empire. And we have a tradition more of self-reliance than of community engagement. Moreover, a plan to reduce the emission of greenhouse gases is forestalled here by suspicion of "big government," egged on by big economic interests that don't want to be regulated.

In the face of the challenges it has taken aboard, the Transition Movement will succeed at the very least in raising consciousness, in part because it suggests tangible constructive action. With each row of vegetables planted and each solar panel installed, it wins the right to say, "Oh, this is necessary, but it's also enlivening to do, isn't it?"

What about observers who envision an economic collapse worse than we already have? Thinking the unthinkable, they see people who are shocked at being impoverished, surrounded by machines that don't work and fuel too expensive to use. And who, in many cases, have skills only for life when the machines *did* work; who are angry, depressed, even despairing.

One approach is to try to scare people into action by

highlighting evidence for impending energy deprivation, climate change, and economic hard times. But this often leads to more despair or, to avoid it, a stronger case of denial.

Michael Brownlee, one of the transition pioneers in the U.S., in an essay published on Carolyn Baker's lively website, says that in some U.S. communities "the effort for relocalization has already essentially stalled." Inspired by the "universe story" told by a Christian writer, after work at a farm and center run by a religious woman, and based on a talk given at Xavier University in Cincinnati, Brownlee's answer is to conclude that the Transition Movement is "all about the Sacred," a point not totally unrelated to Al Gore's framing of climate change as a moral issue.

Perhaps the most effective approach in the U.S. has not yet been developed and, as Brownlee says, the willingness of the Transition Movement to experiment and reinvent itself may lead to a wider success. One job is to help people hear about the challenges soon to be upon us. Another is to find forms of action.

Looking at how Americans feel so entitled, Brownlee concludes "there may be no other nation on the planet where greed and denial are more deeply rooted." While it's understandable that he is driven to denounce the very people he wants to persuade, Brownlee poses the challenge with clarity.

Repeating the observation of a leading environmentalist, Brownlee says that Martin Luther King did not tell the crowd at the Lincoln Memorial "I have a nightmare." King did not need to describe the nightmare because his people were living it. They needed a dream. "But we, I fear, are living a dream," Brownlee continues. "We need to be reminded of the nightmare ahead ... We will never do the things that are needed unless we know the full extent of our predicament."

Here we are back at the basic challenge of the Transition Movement; in England at least, its genius has been to give people something to do together, in the belief that they'd then be more ready to understand the terms of the predicament. Whether more things have to be added to the mix will become clear as the movement evolves.

# CHAPTER 11

# The Mankind Project

*While working as a psychotherapist, Bill Kauth cofounded the Mankind Project (MKP), which is based on an intensive weekend training followed by integration back into a man's community. Over 50,000 men have graduated from this program all over the world. Here in the Rogue Valley you can run into hundreds of men who have done the training, which includes shadow work and the discovery of a sense of mission.*

**CKC: What does the Mankind Project do?**

**BK:** We initiate men into healthy masculinity, and have been doing this for more than twenty-five years. It's all based around a weekend called the "New Warrior Training Adventure," a rite-of-passage for adult men in which they learn emotional literacy and how to open their hearts; how to be truly conscious men, present to the moment. They also open their hearts to other men. They get to see the pain and the drama of other men in ways they never have before. In this process they go through a descent, an ordeal of the heart, and then a return to the community. Those are the classic components of the initiatory process.

**CKC: Give an example of "emotional literacy."**

**BK:** Emotional literacy is simply knowing our feeling body— knowing when we're scared, sad, angry—and being able, in essence, to witness and be with our feeling body, but not be run by it unconsciously. Each man goes into his own heart and finds what we call a transpersonal mission that doesn't have to do with satisfying the ego-self. It's really about caring for the community, which is the classic purpose of rite-of-passage initiations for men.

**CKC: Does MKP accomplish its mission in only one weekend?**

**BK:** After the training weekend men who have opened their hearts and learned so much need to integrate it into their various lives, so we offer a follow up, what we call an integration group. It's basically a men's support group in which men are trained further in emotional literacy and in conflict resolution, so they can embody those skills and bring them back to their families, their workplaces, and the larger community.

**CKC: What kind of conflict-resolution skills do people learn?**

**BK:** We teach a model that we call "clearing." In the case of a conflict with another man, they learn how to bring it to him with their feeling body active, and the knowledge that they may not have all the truth. It's an inquiry to which they bring their feelings, their judgment, and an openness to hearing the other man.

**CKC: About how many men have been through this training?**

**BK:** We have forty-eight chapters around the world, including more than 50,000 men. We're in South Africa, Australia, New Zealand, and all across Europe, including France and Germany. We went into England very early.

**CKC: How did MKP get started?**

**BK:** That's actually a pretty cool story. After graduate school, I had been doing a lot of Gestalt training, being present to what is. So I had the eyes to see humans as they were developing, part of the necessary skill set to do psychotherapy. I was also tracking the powerful personal growth entities in the culture.

At that time the big example was the women's movement. They were doing these consciousness-raising groups. Week after week they grew and evolved, and over the years they became a significant social force. I identified as a feminist therapist, and in my sessions I had an authentic relationship with my clients—I was not just playing an abstract role.

As a feminist therapist I was invited to attend a conference, and while I was there, in the lobby, something happened to me: I looked around and saw all these beautifully conscious, interdependent humans. I noticed that of the 125 of us, I was the only guy. Something came over me, you could say it was a divine call, and I thought, "Somebody has got to do something for the men." I tried to push it away, but the call was in. I was obsessed from that point on.

I saw my friend Ron Herring, with whom I had done Gestalt work, and I said, "Ron, we have to do something for the men." His reply was, "I don't know what you're talking about, but I like your energy, and I have five sons, so I'm in."

At about the same time I met this fellow named Rick Tosi, who was working for General Motors. What I didn't know, and what became important in our work, is that he had done ten years in the United States Marine Corps. We had been in an emotional, cathartic training program together so I had seen his heart, had seen him sobbing and enraged, doing things that men don't ordinarily show one another. I also spontaneously invited him, and he said "Why would you want to do that, work with men? But I like your energy, so whatever you're up to, I'm in."

That was early in 1984. By late that year, the three of us had spent hours sitting around Tosi's kitchen table cobbling this thing together. Each of us brought a kind of genius, each of us was kind of naïve, and we all hailed from Milwaukee, Wisconsin, of all places.

We didn't know anything about archetypes, about initiation. All we knew is that something had to happen.

When we launched the first training in January, 1985, we called it the "Wild Man Weekend."

## CKC: What is accomplished during the weekend?

**BK:** Once men start opening their hearts, once there is a place safe enough, they love it. "Build it and they will come." What is necessary is a safe container, as we call it. Once there is a safe place for men to come and be authentic, they just love it. It's a huge, huge gift to them, and then to their wives, and their children, and their community. It keeps radiating out.

Each man has a transpersonal mission, which means that at some point in his developmental process, being in support groups, he finds a love with other men that most men have never known before. And there is a kind of stability and sense of fulfillment in that. When the men get to that place, there is nothing to do but give. At the point where they get to feel they want to give, instead of just take, they have their mission right there waiting for them. They start doing projects. They created an initiation for teenagers, they started projects to work with women, men in prison—it goes on and on. We have launched thousands and thousands of amazing giving social projects around the world through our work opening men's hearts.

**CKC: The idea of giving is different from mainline business culture. You are saying that men feel a kind of release and excitement, in this container, with this mission?**

**BK:** Living in a consumerist, taker society is not particularly satisfying for anybody. It's like an addiction. It's like shopping in lieu of living. What we are doing is creating places where men can live and learn to give. As I have observed this movement for twenty-five years, I can see the worldviews within which we live. The obvious one that's coming in is what I call the "giver culture," the next iteration of human worldviews. We've been at the forefront of giving men the opportunity to open their hearts and to experience giving. It becomes what we really want to do.

**CKC: In the MKP environment, what are the basic emotional learnings?**

**BK:** Heart opening is such a big issue, being present, being authentic, knowing who we really are. What makes that significant is we live in a culture that almost trains us *not* to tell the truth about who we really are. We pretend to be more powerful or confident then we really feel. The process of healing those wounds is a process of finding enough trust. I alluded earlier to a "safe space" in which we can speak about our wounding, our shadows, the parts we have not really known before, the feelings that have not been acceptable— such as rage, fear, deep sadness, grief. Almost all of us have those feelings. There's something about modern culture that leads us to do an awful lot of lying about who we are. In a safe group, we can discover the truth.

In indigenous cultures, babies stay right with the mothers for two years, mostly in skin contact. The nurturing continues. Physiologically we need that, but for most of the men in our culture, that has been destroyed. There is a wound that is pre-verbal, so we can't speak it. To heal that one requires being in a safe community. Some of the men's support groups in MKP have gone on for ten, twenty years.

**CKC: When people make fun of drums in the woods, of men having animal names, what do you say?**

**BK:** From the outside it does look funny, like the hats worn by fraternal orders a century ago. But what most people don't know is *why* men gathered in those fraternal orders. In the Industrial Revolution when men began going into mines and factories, they sometimes got killed—in which case their families were abandoned. So the men began gathering together, bonding in a ritual way, and the Elks, the Moose, the Masons, the Odd Fellows, the Knights of Pythias, all emerged during that era as a social safety net: in the event of an accident, their families would be taken care of. Then, as we moved into the next century, the government eventually took over those safety net functions. The old fraternal groups lost part of their reason for being, and became guys in funny hats.

What's really splendid is that the work we are doing now, bonding men's hearts, which also bonds their families, has become very necessary because a lot of our systems are breaking down. Our energy system, our financial system, our medical system, our legal system, have all hit a wall. There has to be a way we can take care of each other, and from that place, create the new culture that I see coming in. I see MKP, the brothers, really well positioned to step into the process of creating this new culture.

**CKC: What are the elements of the new consciousness?**

**BK:** The systems that had been created 100 years ago have stopped working for the consciousness that is now showing up. The transition from the old system to the new culture is going to require people who have an ability to see forward, the ability to be creative. I suggested earlier that each man has a transpersonal mission in life. The ability to open my heart allows me to be right here right now with you, and that allows trust. The new culture coming in is going to be rooted in trust, not in legal sanctions—we are essentially done with that.

We are moving into a culture of the gift. Participants in the Mankind Project have been practicing this for twenty-five years. I think so many of us are ready to step into the leadership. There is another piece in this, which is so beautiful. It hasn't quite manifested yet. There is a way of making a living, a way of taking care of us, by using these skills out in the world. I keep inviting social entrepreneurs, social artists, the men and women who have the necessary skills, to step forward and teach this new way of being in the world.

### CKC: What's next for the Mankind Project? What do you envision?

**BK:** The next iteration is reaching out more broadly, going public, allowing ourselves to be seen for the magnificence of what we have done. Because we have been so focused *in*, we have not taken the time to show the brilliance *of* our transpersonal mission, catalyzing social projects all over the world. Few people know about it.

We also are going to be reaching out to helping professionals who are working with men, particularly in these difficult times of financial contraction. For some, their reason for being is disappearing; suicide rates are up. I hope more men will be going into therapy to help them cope with the changes in the world. (In this book see the section on

"Mentoring & Therapy.") And for therapists to know they can refer these men to MKP to learn a whole new level of trust, then guide them during integration when they get back. We provide a service of transformation for men that allows them to flow in a good way with what is going on in the world, to adapt and care for their families. And I'm hopeful.[10]

**CKC: What is the basis of your hope?**

**BK:** I have mutated from being a doomer to seeing the extraordinary brilliance, confidence, and wisdom of human beings; and the spread of knowledge now with the Internet is clearly unprecedented. We are moving very rapidly into this new culture, and what is interesting is that many new social inventions are coming from people under thirty. Kids and grandkids, they get it, they grew up knowing this.

# Mentoring & Therapy

# CHAPTER 12

# Mentoring in
# The Rose Circle

*Leslie Lanes is one of The Rose Circle cofounders; a volunteer mentor, Cara Walsh, also directs a project on restorative justice.[11]*

**CKC: What is The Rose Circle?**

**LL:** It came out of a group of women who got together and asked, "What can we offer in the way of mentoring for teenage girls in our community?" We had a process of meetings until things started to take shape, and although initially we were interested in mentoring girls, we now have circles for boys as well. We train both men and women, and provide opportunities for mentors in the schools as well as one-on-one mentoring. While each official training group includes about twenty people, we also work with a lot of other people who have not received the formal training who help in many ways.

**CW:** A diversity of mentors provides rich weekend-long trainings where participants learn about different communication styles, conflict resolution styles, and how to deal with real-life situations that come up. We also examine some of the experiences we each had as an adolescent in order to focus on how this may affect our own work as mentors to avoid projecting our own issues onto anyone else.

**CKC: What is the structure of the program, and how does it differ from Boys to Men? (See Chapter 13.)**

**LL:** What we have in common is that we have caring, interested adults who want to offer something to the younger generation. We feel we are brother and sister organizations, and the community element is a very big piece of what we do. There has been such a generation gap, and I think there's a reason many youngsters look with disdain at older people who may observe youth and wonder, "What the heck are they doing?"

But I think it's up to the older generation to take the first step by asking, "Who are you? What are you thinking about? What is a good life for you?" Being careful not to ask, "What should I say to *tell* you how to be?"

I think if older people take this first step, and genuinely want to know about young people, then the youth will look to the adults because they are providing a container for them to be themselves—instead of telling them who they should be.

**CKC: Many adults think their job is to pass on their "wisdom." How does this come up in the training?**

**CW:** I think that thought process is actually a hindrance in mentoring. A real mentor is not someone who tells young people what to do or who passes on their "wisdom," but rather a mentor elicits the young person's *own* wisdom, their own truth and knowing—drawing them out by asking the right questions and allowing them go on their own journeys themselves. The great myth about mentoring is that you must have all the answers, have it all together, but it's not that. It's being there and being a presence.

**LL:** What we highlight is just coming into the present moment with a young person; that what you need to say will come out of your being together, as opposed to coming in with a formula. It's a challenge for everyone, and often a new way of being. It's a new situation, like being here in the TV studio with you—you didn't come with a prepared set of questions.

**CKC: What you are describing is parallel to my own experience in doing this show. At first I thought I had to be very knowledgeable about the topic at hand, but as you say, that assumption can be a hindrance and make it difficult to follow the flow.**

**LL:** And the flow is a big thing in The Rose Circle. Like in our not having a five-year plan, but seeing how the organization is emerging: are we listening to what wants to happen next?

**CKC: How do you apply this same philosophy to you and your colleagues?**

**LL:** We want The Rose Circle to demonstrate that both women and men take care of themselves first. Particularly with women, we find that there is a sense of overwhelm in wanting to offer so much. We feel it's important for there to be balance—taking care of your own family, taking care of yourself, is also important. If you are going to serve in the world, you must come from a place of wholeness, not overwhelm.

**CKC: What do you find is the biggest challenge of being a mentor?**

**CW:** Letting go of the thought or notion that I know how to do it, or that I'm doing it the right way. And showing up with openness, that place of surrender, really listening to the flow of the circle, because often I will come to the group armed with a list of activities to do. After a check-in around the circle, my job is actually to tune in and listen, scrapping a lot of what I brought in that day.

**LL:** In addition to training mentors I also work with a circle of girls, and one of the things I notice, as do other mentors, is that some of the girls don't keep their appointments and may not call to let us know. It's a real challenge for the mentors to give unconditionally. We feel we're giving our time to volunteer, and some of the girls are being rude or irresponsible.

**CKC: What do you do when you feel you may be projecting something from your own earlier experience?**

**CW:** Sometimes I can catch it when it's happening, and sometimes not. It is a matter sometimes of deferring to my co-mentors, especially if I realize that I am getting triggered. Also, we use a whole chain of support where each of us has a research mentor with whom she can process anything that may come up in a circle.

*Later I spoke talk with Ella Riley-Adams and Elizabeth Westmoreland, two girls who participate in Rose Circles:*

**CKC: You have been in the circle how long?**

**ER:** Three years.

**CKC: You're in an unusual situation, in that the mentor for your group is your own mother.**

**ER:** Yes, it's a different dynamic, but it's never been a problem for us, although there have been times when I've asked her to leave the room. We have another mentor who stays when I have to share something that I don't necessarily want my mother to hear.

**CKC: How do girls in the circle talk differently than they would, say, in the school cafeteria?**

ER: The main difference is that people are listening more closely. When we are talking in the cafeteria it is more of a back-and-forth, a bit more chaotic. In the circle we are focusing on the speaker.

**CKC: What do your friends, who are not in the circle, ask you about?**

EW: "Is it like a club or something? Can I be in it?"

**CKC: After the Mankind Project training weekend participants are not supposed to talk about exactly what was done, but participants can talk about the effect it had on them.**

ER: That's mostly what confidentiality means for us as well. It's not much of an issue for me because my mom is in the circle, as a mentor, but if she were not, I could only say, "I talked about so-and-so" and "I felt this way," but I couldn't talk about other people's experiences.

**CKC: What difference does the circle make in your life?**

ER: On the practical side, being in the circle has made me more okay with public speaking. Because I have the experience of sharing my feelings with a group of other girls with whom I'm close, it makes me more okay with sharing things with other groups of people. Also, circle has made me more aware of myself.

EW: That's also what I would say. Just being able to know what my feelings are and *why* I'm feeling that way, to identify it, helps with any problems I may be having.

**CKC: What would be an example?**

ER: Sometimes when I'm wondering why I'm feeling really stressed out, or sad, I think back and realize my mother said something to me on Monday that affected the whole week.

**CKC: What would it be like to be in a school where everyone was in a circle?**

EW: I think it would connect everyone a lot better, help everyone to be closer and more understanding. In circle, we learn to resolve differences. If everyone had these tools we could communicate a lot more easily.

**CKC: In a film made about Boys to Men called *Journeyman*, two of the boys interviewed point out that adult men are scared of teenage boys, which the local director explained is "because they remember times when there was a lot of conflict."**

ER: Because my mother is involved, I've been to several meetings for mentors in The Rose Circle and heard many women say, "I wish this had existed when I was growing up." I think it's really cool that we do have circles at this time in our lives.

*Now we meet Ella's mother, Renee Riley-Adams, who is a Rose Circle mentor:*

**CKC: What gave you the idea for doing this mentoring?**

RR: I came to a meeting for mentors, but was unsure if I would be involved because I had a lot of other things going on. But when someone said, "Let's start a pilot circle—who knows some girls?" I had to raise my hand, because a couple of days prior one mother I know got into my car outside the school and said, "We need to do something for the girls, because the boys are calling them 'bitches' and they are not doing anything about it. We need to do a mother-daughter circle or something."

There's a lot of name-calling that goes around like that; it's cool in this culture where rap music lyrics include "bitches and hoes" [a way of saying "whores"]. When my daughter was a freshman, one of the dances off campus was called, "Office Ho's and CEOs." What's *that* about?

**CKC: If part of the job of being a parent is to socialize the child, how does that differ from being a mentor?**

**RR:** It is very different. I've been a teacher in the past, now I am a parent and a circle mentor. In circle there is no agenda: we deal with whatever comes up. We do have various topics, usually chosen by the girls, but sometimes we just ask, "What's important to you?" Or we might say, "We have heard people talk about X, so do you want to talk about that?"

Usually my co-mentor and I discuss a topic, and think of a way forward. When we did a circle on cyberspace, I introduced it with an online video. Sometimes we have role-playing. And although we may think of a theme for circle, if we don't get to that topic it's fine: we let it go. It depends on what is emerging in that particular circle— that's very different from teaching, where I had certain things to get across.

Circle is a chance for the girls to be who they are, in the moment. And one of the biggest gifts of the circle is when people find out they are not alone. "I have this problem with my parents (or boyfriend, or whomever). Does anyone else have this problem? How have you dealt with it?" Not really asking for answers, but just wanting to sit with a problem.

CHAPTER 13

# Boys to Men

*In Africa there's a saying, "If we don't initiate the boys, they will burn down the village," but our society lacks a consistent and effective ritual of initiation, while at the same time some boys are growing up without the regular presence of a father. With the question arising, "How do our boys become men?" one answer is provided by a movement called Boys to Men.[12] Pete Young, the local director, and Keb Bales, one of the boys who has been through the program and helped to staff many trainings, spoke with me about the program in Southern Oregon.*

**CKC: Pete, can you tell us a little about Boys to Men?**

**PY:** Our Southern Oregon program is made up of four trainings. The first, for the mentors, is a powerful program about regressing back to a time when we were youth, using that wisdom as a resource in mentoring—and youth like Keb are an important part of that training. Then we have a training for boys nine to twelve, called the Raven Training, which Keb has also done and later staffed a number of times. For ages thirteen to seventeen we have the Rite-of-Passage Adventure, after which young men achieve the status of "Journeymen." When they get to the age of seventeen or eighteen, we initiate them—it no longer makes sense to call them journeymen. They are now men, and join us in a circle. At that point often they go off to college.

**CKC: I know someone in his eighties who has gone through your training for mentors and has said it was one of the most important experiences of his life, that there were things he thought he had dealt with but discovered that he had not, and that he was now able to.**

**PY:** I think I know who you are talking about, he came on fire, and that's actually the nature of mentoring. The first step is to revisit old woundings, which makes it possible to respond to young people who are going through something similar. Our wounds give us a certain perspective on life, and age gives us an opportunity to process them. Working with young people gives us another opportunity.

**CKC: Keb, when you originally went through the program, what was the most important thing to you and how did it change you?**

**KB:** It gave me a sense of responsibility. When I first went there, I felt very isolated. What it did was change how I looked at things. At first I felt alone and in pain, but I realized I was not alone. The program helps you look at other people and feel united with them.

**CKC: How was it to be with the mentors?**

**KB:** I guess an important part of it was that you see seventy-year-old men running around playing Capture the Flag with you. Everyone's having fun, everyone's playing. You get the feeling of being more mature, more like an adult, but you still have that inner child piece of you.

**PY:** We compartmentalize our lives: we come home from work and watch TV, and we suffer alone. We compartmentalize by age. It's really tragic. With our program, young men see us, older men, enjoying each other and they become part of that. There's a lot of healing there.

**CKC: Keb, what were the surprises for you in spending a weekend with these older men and with your peers?**

**KB:** It changes from the Ravens age group to the Journeymen, although when I was first going through the program I wasn't quite sure what to think. It makes you feel good but you don't know why. Now that I'm older, and a staff member who is considered to be one of the "old guys" (at least according to an eight-year-old), I feel a sense of responsibility with having people look up to me.

**CKC: What's the closest we have to an initiation for men?**

**PY:** I've heard men speak of military experiences as initiatory; the death of a parent initiates a new phase of life for children. Michael Meade talks about initiations happening *all* the time. Gangs require you to do something to prove yourself. But there needs to be a community and mentors to make the initiation meaningful. Without community, initiation is somewhat hollow. Locally, we try to create community, and the program ends in an initiation into manhood. I think classic initiation requires a letting go of the old; moving into the new after going into a dark, challenging place and emerging with renewed purpose and intention in life.

**CKC: Sounds a bit like the Mankind Project which, I take it, has been very important in starting Boys to Men.**

**PY:** It was certainly important to me in my life, but has also been important in Boys to Men. Many of the volunteers have been New Warrior men looking to find some alternative for youth.

**CKC: Keb, what do think you would have missed if this program did not exist?**

**KB:** The most important part of this program for me was that there were people there who were mentoring me. Your father and mother of course respect you as their child, but not necessarily as a young, independent man. A good mentor sees you as someone who is growing, someone who is trying to be his own person, someone trying to discover who he is. I don't know how to answer the question of where would I be today without the program, but I am guessing I would not be in as good a place.

**CKC: Pete, what is the challenge of the program for people initiating and running it?**

**PY:** To find an ample supply of boys and young men, and to find men who are willing to step up and become mentors. The program could expand dramatically, given the need, if we had more mentors.

**CKC: The training makes the point that a lot of men are afraid of teenage boys. Why is this the case?**

**PY:** Most of our own experience of being teenagers was pretty terrifying. It's a time of insecurity, of looking to find our ideals, and ridicule is the most toxic thing a teenager can face. But that is what happens a lot. I have heard many men say they do not want to look at their teenage years again: it's just scary.

How do we interact with teenagers? The model that we have in our culture doesn't work, including ridicule, which is a poison. Boys to Men does work, but until you know how to be a mentor it feels challenging to step back into that place. Sensitive respect is the nourishing food. How to do that is to inquire, to be curious. Suspend judgment, suspend having to be the one who has the answer, and allow the young men to reflect and explore. It's such a powerful process, one of honoring, and not one that most young people experience because adults are so ready to be the "answer people."

**CKC: Keb, what kinds of questions do your friends who have not gone into the program ask you about it?**

**KB:** They rarely ask, but when they do it's something like "What do you do?" or "What was it like?" If I tried to answer I would have to say it was like being "hit by a shovel" in the sense of having to change the direction of my life.

**CKC: Given that the process is a secret, to be experienced rather than read about, what can you say about what you are asked to do?**

**KB:** Pete, can I talk about "Crossing the Line"?

**PY:** Yes.

**KB:** There is a line drawn in the sand and everyone stands on one side of it, then a series of questions is asked. If your answer is "yes," you cross the line.

**PY:** The intention here is to show that the human experience includes a variety of challenges. We all have pain and suffering at times, joy at other times, and although the boys come from many different backgrounds—racially, for example—having challenges is part of being human.

But we do ask for a level of confidentiality, for example, when sharing our own process. And we don't want to tell the boys in advance "on Friday night we do this." The boys are certainly allowed to tell their parents about everything that happens, but for other boys that come through, we'd rather have it be a surprise for them.

CHAPTER 14

# From Grief to Joy

After loss, Francis Weller advises, find other people with whom to express your grief. This is not the time for self-reliance. It hurts to keep grief private. Mourning with social support leads to the possibility of joy. That is the basic message in his book, *The Wild Edge of Sorrow: Rituals of Renewal and the Sacred Work of Grief.*

As a psychotherapist Weller helps clients go beyond the U.S. pattern of friends saying, only a brief interval after the loss, "put it behind you." And as a workshop leader, he arranges the equivalent of a village to support, at least briefly, a member who has suffered a loss.

In the nine poetic and often counterintuitive chapters of *The Wild Edge of Sorrow*, Weller is inspired in part by the insights of great psychologists such as C.G. Jung, as well as by the long-time pattern of humans having evolved in tribes and villages, within which our ancestors could share grief.

He was helped in the latter by co-teaching with Malidoma Somé, who comes from a country in West Africa where people still live in tribes and villages. Weller learned the former, the psychology, while earning two masters degrees at John F. Kennedy University.

Weller sees the U.S. as a culture that encourages mainly the upward journey (or as the state of New York says in its motto, "excelsior"). But as shamanic cultures know, it is the downward journey that makes it possible to move into joy and, as his subtitle says, "renewal."

Weller has brought his message to the men's movement, to patients with terminal cancer, to observers who are able to see the "ongoing destruction of our planet," as well as to private clients, and he has observed an increased willingness to move into public grief. In his own training Weller initially found it hard to express his grief in public, but hugely rewarding once, as he says, "the dam broke."

Weller uses the metaphor of "gates" with regard to grief. He discusses five of them, starting with the gate of what Buddhists call impermanence; followed by the gate of "places that have not known love"; then the sorrows of the world; dashed expectations; and finally "ancestral grief."

The author knows there are even more gates into grief, one being trauma—whether suffered in war or sexual abuse, for example. If we ever notice an end to progress (for many, purchasing power stagnated decades ago), that would be another gate.

Like so much else, grief has been in the closet, either denied or not quite ready for prime time. Weller's reference to "a layer of silence" reminds me of when I once met a veteran of World War Two at a party and asked him about his experience in Europe. He said he had never talked about it, in part because no one who could understand had ever asked him and really wanted to listen. It was then forty years after the end of that war. (Disclosure: I should add that Weller wrote the Foreword to my book *Gift of Darkness*, the first volume of The Gratitude Trilogy, the second being *Enlarging Our Comfort Zones*.)

In our culture it's counterintuitive to think that, as Weller puts it, stories of sorrow shared in a group could possibly be "rituals of renewal." The author quotes Joanna Macy's assertion that "The heart that breaks open can contain the whole universe." When I first heard that claim, working in citizen diplomacy as Macy and her late husband Fran did, I was skeptical. How would dwelling on sorrow lead to anything positive? I was wrong, and especially in this culture, I'm not the only one.

Francis Weller's book on "the wild edge of sorrow" represents a challenge to denial, whether of loss or dangers, and a celebration of working together rather than singly. Above all, it offers an entry to what he calls "the healing ground."

CHAPTER 15

# Taking PTSD Seriously

A rtists and communities are paying increasing attention
to post-traumatic stress disorder. For example, my town
has conducted a homecoming event for vets, including a
workshop for a group of them, followed by a large public
welcome, at which workshop participants read their poems.
One speaker emptied his pack of many clattering containers
of prescription meds and jokingly asked the shocked
audience, "Anybody want to party?" He then said he was
taking the pills "for your protection." The whole process is
shown in a superb documentary, *The Welcome*, produced by
Bill McMillan and Kim Shelton (Chapter 19).

My town also has an annual New Plays Festival, and
in 2014 the first piece was *Homecoming* by Michael Edan,
a playwright from New York State. He lets us listen to a
disabled vet returning from Iraq and interacting with his
wife, parents, and a long-time buddy. At night over a bottle
of scotch, the son opens up and starts telling his dad, a
Vietnam vet, what it was like in Iraq:

"This one time after shooting rockets into a building
that we were receiving heavy gun fire from, we stormed in.
There's two teenage kids, a child and another guy—probably
the father but it was hard to tell cause half his face was
missing—all dead. The woman bleeding from her head
was screaming 'Why? *Laish, laish.*' I'm with the corpsman
trying to help her while the rest of the marines are going

through the building; and something snapped. I felt like I was going nuts and just lost it, started to cry. The woman came up and touched my cheek. She kept saying *'Insha Allah,* God's will'—cause the people there, it doesn't matter what s**t happens, somehow they accept it as God's will. But it wasn't God's will, it was my f**king will. I gave the order that killed her family."

According to the official Veterans Administration (VA) website, symptoms of PTSD can include "worry or anxiety, anger, sadness or hopelessness, sleep problems, trauma reminders, avoidance of stressful situations, disconnection from people, disconnection from reality…" Of course, as with every other psychiatric syndrome, some false claims occur, but PTSD has become a major problem.

The true cost of war thus includes not only the sending of a military force, the building of bases, the bribery of foreign officials, the physical casualties on both sides, and the debt incurred, but also the care of vets when they return with such psychiatric troubles as PTSD. Often the damage is long lasting. One of the VA programs for vets returning from Iraq and Afghanistan also served vets from Vietnam, a war that ended in 1975, and that began, for the U.S., in 1961, more than a half century ago.

PTSD affects not only a vet but also his or her family. It also affects friends, community, and co-workers (if he or she has found a job). Whether it is sleeping with a handgun under the pillow, suffering nightmares and anxiety attacks, or doing violence to the family or self (twenty-two returning vets commit suicide every day, according to a study covering 1999–2010). PTSD can ruin a family, a career, a life.

Many artists have depicted the phenomenon of trauma in vets. Along with the documentary *Coming Home,* and the gripping Edan play, there is David Finkel's brilliantly reported book *Thank You for Your Service.*

Meanwhile, the tendency to deny or push aside the true cost of things can be illustrated by the following analogy: How much does our gasoline cost? We can't drive by a filling station without seeing the current price on a large sign. But that price doesn't include the cost of military efforts to secure "access" to oil fields, or the health costs of pollution from vehicles, much less the slowly accumulating damage from greenhouse gases. It doesn't include what President Obama has called "wasteful subsidies" to the oil companies, or tax breaks.

Economists call hidden costs "externalities." It would be interesting to know how much of the "profit" in various enterprises comes from costs that are paid, eventually, by the public, or not paid fully at all except in the suffering of too many private individuals.

PTSD is not adequately treated for at least two reasons: soldiers are often reluctant to ask for or accept help, and the dominant protocol for that help may not be the best we can do. Soldiers (or "warriors") are taught to be tough, and nothing is worse for a young male soldier than the "uss" words—to be called a "wuss" or a "pussy." Suck it up and get well, what's the problem?

This attitude was memorably expressed by hard-right radio personality Michael Savage:

"If the whole nation is told, 'Boo-hoo-hoo, come and get a medication, come and get treatment, talk about mental illness,' you know what you wind up with? You wind up with Obama in the White House and liars in every phase of the government... A weak, sick, broken nation. And you need men like me to save the country. You need men to stand up and say stop crying like a baby over everything. Stand up already. Stop telling me how sick you are and sad you are. Talk about the good things in your life."

The dominant method of treatment for PTSD is called "habituation," which involves the vet describing the traumatic scene again and again. A soldier may start by resisting the prompt to revisit the traumatic event and end, in theory, being bored by his or her own account. That is the hope.

One project that emphasizes feeling good while recalling trauma is run by Michael Mithoefer, M.D., who uses the drug called MDMA (a.k.a. "Ecstasy") as an adjunct to therapy. By itself, feeling love for a few hours might be transitory, but Mithoefer's finding is that effects of therapy done while the client is in this state can last.

Careful long-term studies are moving MDMA from being banned as a rave drug to being legal as prescription medicine. New research shows its effectiveness, as an adjunct to psychotherapy, in cases of post-traumatic stress disorder that have been resistant to other treatments.

Specifically, a small scale but long-term study of sixteen "subjects" showed definite improvement, and no drawbacks, after an average length of time of forty-five months following treatment. None of the participants developed a drug dependency, and none suffered cognitive impairment, which were two of the fears associated with earlier reporting about MDMA.

Supported by the Multidisciplinary Association for Psychedelic Studies (MAPS), the research was conducted by scientists in South Carolina, including principal investigator Michael Mithoefer. MAPS seeks to restore MDMA to the medicine chest of psychiatrists, a use it once had before being banned in the U.S. in 1985.

Pharmaceutical drugs, which are legal, are profitable to the firms that develop and market them but don't work in many cases. The Mithoefer study focuses not on a random sample of PTSD patients, but on people who were resistant to other treatments—in other words, on some of the hardest cases.

People with PTSD include victims of rape and soldiers who have been the victims of improvised explosive devices (IEDS) or other attacks. The Mithoefer study included both categories. Some of the sufferers had flashbacks of the distressing episode for years, a condition that could be not only unpleasant but debilitating as well. The average length of time from the traumatic incident to the treatment was nineteen years.

MDMA has been experienced by millions of users, both before and after Federal officials made it illegal. However, after July 1, 1985, psychiatrists could not continue to use the molecule without risking their license to practice.

In sponsoring this research, MAPS examined the argument not that the drug can enhance life for "normals," but that it can act as a medicine to help restore damaged people's health. In short, the MAPS campaign does not rely on a critique of "normality," which has been offensive to folks who had never experienced anything else. Rather, the investigators decided to focus on people who were the victims of a crime (rape) or a battlefield (IEDs) and who, with their long-suffering partners, just wanted to be free from nightmares and other flashbacks.

# Mindful Molecules

# Section Introduction

S ocial inventors need several skills: among them is the ability to think outside the box. Anything that can help people do this is potentially helpful. One possibility is psychedelics, which since the 1960s have been demonized by some, praised to the heavens by others, generally suppressed rather than studied scientifically.

However, before the panic, some promising research was accomplished and, since the panic, research has been supported to the extent possible in the U.S. and abroad by organizations such as Rick Doblin's MAPS, the Heffter Research Institute, and Bob Jesse's Council on Spiritual Practices, along with Amanda Feilding's Beckley Foundation in the UK.

Before the government panic about "drugs," a Stanford professor of engineering ran a research program in the 1960s on using classic psychedelics to promote creativity. He and his team recruited qualified professionals with problems they wanted to solve, gave them mindful molecules, and studied the results. The subjects were mentally healthy. They volunteered. They had expert guidance during the experiments. The drugs were of known purity. The environment was safe.

What the scientists found was that under these conditions, the molecules increased creativity.

However, this research program fell victim to anti-drug propaganda that failed to distinguish between drugs that are addictive or otherwise dangerous and certain molecules that have been shown to increase creativity. For example, methamphetamine is dangerous. It causes brain damage. It is widely used, alas.

Some other molecules, also called psychedelics, have been used for centuries in ritual settings. Examples include mescaline (found in some cactus plants), psilocybin (from certain mushrooms), and DMT (present in ayahuasca, a plant-based medicine from what is now Latin America). According to peer-reviewed papers, these molecules are not additive or otherwise harmful, when pure psychedelics are used in appropriate amounts, in safe settings, with expert guidance.

This section reports on the wise use of psychedelics. In this book, the context is social invention.

# CHAPTER 16

# The Sixties and Afterward

I t is tempting to assume we have learned everything we need to about the Sixties, and to leave safely submerged what cannot be re-floated ("Thank God," say some). But here are two books that remind us about questions that were raised then—and that are arising again, buoyed in part by legal but quiet research conducted abroad as well as here in the U.S.

I've been following this re-emergence neither as a devotee of the war on drugs nor as an old hippie (I am an elder, but was never a hippie); rather, as a former board member of the Council on Spiritual Practices,[14] a group organized by Robert Jesse and "dedicated to making direct experience of the sacred more available to more people."

One evening in winter 1967, I was just a tourist lucky enough to witness Jim Morrison of The Doors on stage at San Francisco's Fillmore Auditorium, instructing his "baby" to set the night on fire. As a relentlessly single-minded graduate student then, I watched as Timothy Leary, dressed in a white Nehru outfit and grinning broadly, twirled a long strand of glass beads under a strobe light, his teeth flashing on and off.

What is the benefit, decades later, of revisiting the melodrama initiated by a Harvard psychologist eating bitter, stringy psilocybin mushrooms in Cuernavaca in summer 1960? Admittedly the cast of characters soon included Allen Ginsberg, Aldous Huxley, and the comparative religionist Huston Smith; and the settings, a prestigious university, an isolated Mexican beach town, and a patrician Hudson Valley estate—the story certainly boasted cinematic potential. However, the main benefit for us is that the Harvard group was presented with many of the questions that illegality soon froze like actors in a prolonged tableau, questions now twitching back to public life.

Like Jay Stevens' earlier book *Storming Heaven*, Don Lattin's *Harvard Psychedelic Club* is a wry look at this tumultuous history. But whereas the former covers a wider scope ("LSD and the American Dream"), the latter focuses sharply on the group that began in Cambridge.

And, in contrast to Lattin's account, Gary Bravo's *Birth of a Psychedelic Culture* brings us the ruminations of two of the surviving principals of the Harvard group: the scholarly Ralph Metzner and the psychologist formerly known as Richard Alpert, who transmogrified into the spiritual teacher Ram Dass. Their recorded conversation has the flavor of a lively reunion as the two recall an astonishing young adulthood, generously illustrated with snapshots and brief statements from colleagues.

As Metzner acknowledged in his own *The Ecstatic Adventure*, the Harvard group generated *a* psychedelic culture—not the first, not the only. For example, Huxley had published a couple of books in the Fifties on thoughts occasioned by psychedelics in that capacious mind of his. The investment banker Gordon Wasson had written at length in *Life* about his discovery of a psilocybin ritual in Oaxaca. Stan Grof had done extensive research with LSD therapy in Prague and in the U.S.; as had Abram Hoffer and Humphry Osmond, in Canada.

The main question raised by reminders of the Harvard cohort is this: What are the benefits, if any, of various psychoactive molecules? Should the group's saga be dismissed as a swirl of inflated claims and false hopes, or can it also be read as a set of questions raised and, in some cases, not yet satisfactorily answered?

Let us deal first with the charismatic Leary. According to an unforgiving obituary in Harvard's university daily, he had likened himself to Prometheus, presumably for having set minds on fire. In the same spirit of grandiosity, Leary might also be compared with Martin Luther, in the sense of challenging the establishment of his day and suggesting direct access to another reality—in Luther's case through his translation of the Bible; in Leary's, through a molecule that he wanted to help make vernacular. One difference is that despite the best efforts of activists, Leary was unable to get enough political power on his side to weather the inevitable counter-revolution.

It is a cliché of the underground psychedelic culture that Leary was advised by Huxley to continue discreet research among patients, artists, intellectuals, and the like; by Ginsberg, to turn on as many people as possible. (The poet's advice came during an acid initiation when Ginsberg sought to get JFK and Khrushchev on the phone in order to settle the nuclear standoff.)

However, by the early Sixties, whatever Leary would do, the cat was clawing its way out of the bag, and by the later Sixties the West Coast contingent led by Ken Kesey was sponsoring "acid tests," at which lysergic acid diethylamide-25 (LSD) was widely distributed. This drug is famously potent, and millions of doses were available through the grace of such underground chemists as Stanley Owsley. Word of mouth would have assured its spread, even without the McLuhanesque slogan of "Tune in, turn on, drop out." Even without Leary's claim, in a *Playboy* interview, that

LSD was the "most powerful aphrodisiac ever discovered by man."

In any case, far from dwindling, the list of psychoactive molecules used in the U.S. continues to grow. Whereas the Harvard "club" relied mainly on psilocybin and LSD, many "psychonauts" have since become familiar with such drugs as *ayahuasca* from the Amazon basin, *ibogaine* from West Africa, *salvia divinorum* from Mexico.

3,4-Methylenedioxymethamphetamine (MDMA, also known as Ecstasy; or as Metzner dubbed it, an "empathogen") was rediscovered in a California lab and became a staple first of psychotherapy and then of the underground rave culture.

And, in what may serve as a portent, ayahuasca "tea" is now actually legal in the U.S., at least for adherents of a religion that started in Brazil, as is mescaline for members of the Native American Church.

Meanwhile, a publication as hardheaded as *The Economist*, eager to stop the drug wars, claims that "Prohibition has failed; legalization is the least-bad solution." Legalization, the editorial continues, "...would transform drugs from a law-and-order problem into a public health problem, which is how they ought to be treated."

Misuse is certainly a problem, as are addictive drugs such as the widespread methamphetamine. But to what extent are certain molecules, properly used by mentally healthy people, a problem at all? The Harvard club clearly treated psychedelics as an opportunity, although now, with the wisdom of hindsight, various questions arise:

- In what ways are psychoactive drugs useful for dealing with alcoholism and other addictions, terminal cancer, and what we now call post-traumatic stress disorder (PTSD)?

- In what situations do psychedelics actually involve danger, including the cost of trivialization? How do these compare with other dangers that we accept—such as driving or consuming alcohol—and how can the dangers in using psychedelics be avoided or minimized?

- Under what conditions, if any, are psychedelics beneficial not only for medical purposes but also for "expanding consciousness" and occasioning "spiritual" experiences?

- What are good models for a search that might appropriately use psychedelics? (Leary and Metzner devised a manual for psychedelic sessions based loosely on a Tibetan classic and wrote a paper praising Hermann Hesse as a pioneer, especially in the novels *Steppenwolf* and *Journey to the East*.)

- If guides are necessary or helpful, how should they be chosen? Who will train them, what should they do and avoid doing? Should psychedelics be used to reinforce commitments already made, as to a specific religious belief?

- Should powerful drugs be legalized, or decriminalized, and who will control access?

- Over the long term, how can the effect of psychedelics be channeled to positive ends? To what extent does this require a continuing practice that's not dependent on drugs?

- If people undertake a "spiritual" journey, how can they best deal with the vicissitudes of a relationship with a guru, "spiritual friend," or counselor?

- For those who believe that a major cultural or spiritual change is necessary, can any of these molecules help, and if so under what conditions? (Huxley believed a psychoactive drug had a place in the utopia about which he wrote in *Island*.)

I gather that psychedelic enthusiasts long ago got past the fantasy of dumping LSD in reservoirs and hoping for world peace. In its place, researchers are now legally studying the effects of the drugs, both as medicines and, as Roland Griffiths at Johns Hopkins writes, occasions for "mystical-type experiences."

For example, with help from the Council on Spiritual Practices, the Hopkins research team reported that 33 percent of volunteers "rated the psilocybin experience as being the single most spiritually significant experience of his or her life," with an additional 38 percent rating it to be "among the top five most spiritually significant experiences."

With support from the Multidisciplinary Association for Psychedelic Studies (MAPS), legal research on several psychoactive drugs is now being or has been conducted in such countries as Canada, Germany, Israel, Russia, Switzerland, and at several universities in the U.S. (For more details, visit www.maps.org) MAPS itself is now focusing on medical uses of marijuana and on MDMA, especially as it may help with post-traumatic stress disorder, widespread among rape and accident victims and among vets returning from Iraq and Afghanistan (as reported in Chapter 15).

So far, most of this global research falls within the medical model. But the brooding omnipresence hovering above the field remains the experiment at Marsh Chapel, the last effort of the Harvard group before they decamped from the Boston area. A graduate student named Walter Pahnke conducted a study on a Good Friday, based on an elaborate set of criteria, finding that 30–40 percent of volunteers had a "complete" mystical experience with the help of psilocybin.

In *Cleansing the Doors of Perception,* Huston Smith, a participant at Marsh Chapel, went so far as to write: "Until the Good Friday Experiment, I had no direct personal encounter with God of the sort that *bhakti yogis,* Pentecostals, and born-again Christians describe." The son of missionaries in China and a believer belonging to a mainline Protestant church, Smith wrote a best-selling book about the principal religions of the world. A "mystical-type" experience might be experienced as "Christian," as "Hindu," or whatever; and it can also be received without the hypothesis of any god.

Five decades after the Harvard "psychedelic club," that university was again somewhat involved with psychedelics, not only as the alma mater of the persistent and ingenious Rick Doblin, founder of MAPS, but as the base for research, for example, on peyote as a sacrament in the Native American Church.

If the main benefit of psychedelics is a glimpse beyond consensus reality—the personal discovery that "there are more things in heaven and earth than are dreamt of in your philosophy"—then we deserve careful research on what they can, in fact, make possible. In science it's true that Kary Mullis credits LSD with helping to spark his Nobel Prize-winning discovery of polymerase chain reaction (PCR), but despite rumors about Francis Crick, most Nobels have been awarded for work that, to the best of our knowledge, was done on no drugs more psychedelic than coffee, beer, or tobacco.

Meanwhile Michael Schrage (research fellow at MIT), in his column in *Fortune* magazine, made a case for the use of psychedelics to generate creative thought among business people. Schrage imagined a retreat center for "creative business visualization," at which visiting executive teams would be given "small, precise dosages" of psychoactive materials to "push themselves beyond the boundaries of conventional business perception" and thus gain a competitive edge in the global marketplace.

In considering whether psychedelics, optimally used, can reveal other ways of thinking and experiencing the world, the Hopkins research and *Fortune* column went far beyond a medical model which asks mainly whether a drug can do more good than harm in curing a disease. In contrast, the basic question raised by the Harvard group was this: Under what circumstances can psychedelics liberate humans from restrictions normal in the everyday thinking that is necessary for such challenges as designing bridges, driving cars, and completing tax returns? And in what ways, to what extent, under what conditions, can some of these molecules help to enrich our lives?

The Harvard "club" began proposing and exploring models. Whatever the aftermath in the Sixties (or as a physician would say, the "sequelae"), it was in the best tradition of a university to raise the questions. Now we are gradually finding other opportunities to propose answers, and on that basis, to improve public policy.

CHAPTER 17

# Guided Psychedelic Sessions

What might the optimal use of psychedelics be, not only in curing human maladies but also in enhancing human capabilities? This is the question considered by Jim Fadiman, a Stanford Ph.D. in psychology, in his book *The Psychedelic Explorer's Guide: Safe, Therapeutic, and Sacred Journeys.*

Fadiman believes that psychedelic molecules such as lysergic acid diethylamide (LSD) are potential blessings cast into the shadows by hysteria in the 1960s and thus almost wholly lost to legal use, and to science, for more than half a century. The question, he implies, is not whether the molecules will nonetheless be ingested, but the extent to which they will be optimally used (or at least, as scientists would say, "non-trivially").

With Willis Harman, then a professor at Stanford and later head of the Institute for Noetic Sciences, Fadiman did pioneering research on the enhancement of creativity through guided psychedelic sessions. The subjects were not "hippies" but engineers, architects, and other professionals who were asked to bring difficult problems on which they were working. On a continuum from recreational use to the kind of blazing spiritual experience described by Stan Grof and hundreds of others, this would fall somewhere between the extremes. Helping engineers solve problems sounds more socially productive than having a good time, less dramatic than shifting an entire worldview.

Along with organizations such as the Multidisciplinary Association for Psychedelic Studies and the Council on Spiritual Practices, both headquartered in northern California, Fadiman has gathered detailed guidelines for people who choose to take psychedelics and those who guide them. His larger purpose, he says, is to enhance human capabilities.

Fadiman's book tells several stories, all deeply engaging, with the first being practical advice about how to set up and run an optimal session. (Fadiman's own "first trip" was guided by Richard Alpert, who later became Ram Dass; and among the people Fadiman has guided is Stewart Brand, who started the *Whole Earth Catalog*.) While not advising anyone to take drugs, Fadiman has helped people who have chosen to ingest these substances to have the best possible experience.

*The Psychedelic Explorer's Guide* also shares brief excerpts from trip reports by pioneers such as the author Aldous Huxley; Rabbi Zalman Schachter, founder of the Jewish Renewal movement; and Huston Smith, author of *The World's Religions*.

In his book, Fadiman considers the many possibilities for providing faster and more effective therapy with the help of psychedelics and other drugs. Some returning vets and many others suffer from post-traumatic stress disorder (PTSD), and current research suggests a role for psychedelic-assisted therapy. (See Chapter 15.)

And, not unlike the current research at Johns Hopkins on mystical-like experiences on psychedelics, Fadiman explores the "sacred" possibilities.

I gather that what Fadiman would like to have happen is the training of a network of entheoguides modeled on best practices, but not controlled by political entities that rule by fear and which, in a democracy, must answer to people whose fear they inspire.

While the book is predominantly by Fadiman, it also includes chapters by other scholars and thinkers such as Alan Watts, Willis Harman, and George Leonard (author, with Michael Murphy of Esalen, of *The Life We are Given*).

Along with dispelling an assortment of myths and misconceptions, *The Psychedelic Explorer's Guide: Safe, Therapeutic, and Sacred Journeys* awakens many questions that flared briefly in the 1960s.

CHAPTER 18

# Manifesting Minds

M*anifesting Minds,* an anthology from the Multi-disciplinary Association for Psychedelic Studies (MAPS), describes some of the positive uses of what a friend calls "mindful molecules." In contrast to both the war on drugs and across-the-board legalization, MAPS recommends prescription medicine status for classic psychedelics such as psilocybin and ayahuasca, as well as other psychoactive substances such as marijuana and MDMA.

This would be one middle way between free-for-all legalization and the prohibition that started under President Nixon and has led, MAPS argues, to an era of false official information, criminal enterprises, and impure street drugs. Physicians would prescribe these substances, which would then be purchased at a pharmacy.

*Manifesting Minds,* co-edited by Rick Doblin, a Kennedy School graduate who started MAPS in 1986, and by his colleague Brad Burge, has its origins in material that previously appeared in the *MAPS Bulletin,* a magazine that is sent to members and has included a dazzling array of articles.

During the decades when society has generally been barred from the careful and legal use of pure psychedelics, MAPS has supported research on the use of mindful molecules in the treatment of a variety of ailments, including post-traumatic stress disorder and anxiety about dying from a disease such as cancer.

Like most other collections, there is a bit of unevenness (the Aldous Huxley interview, for example, is less than his very best statement), but the general level is high and the book contains many gems that help in the mission of addressing the core question: "Why use this stuff, and in what ways?"

For example, one early section discusses coming of age. It's no secret that millions of high school and college students have not found it difficult to "experiment," but this book offers heartwarming stories of parents who have initiated their own offspring, teaching patterns of what they consider wise use, in some cases sharing carefully arranged experiences. Other sections focus on the arts, medicine, psychotherapy, sexuality, spirituality, ecology, and technology.

Near the end of his life, Terence McKenna co-initiated the All Chemical Arts Conference in 1999 on the Big Island of Hawaii. Like *Manifesting Minds,* the conference described positive uses of mindful molecules, and was addressed by some of the same people who also appear in the MAPS book—including novelist Tom Robbins and Mark Pesce, co-inventor of virtual reality markup language (VRML).

At the risk of appearing less omniscient than reviewers often pretend to be, I confess to learning much, even from early sections of this book. Perhaps if I were an extreme athlete, I would have known, before being instructed by James Oroc, that low levels of psychedelics are routinely used by many mountain climbers, paraglider pilots, skiers, and surfers, to improve, they believe, balance, endurance, and reflexes. I was dazzled as a child by *Fantasia,* but perhaps if I had followed independent films more closely, I would have seen many of the psychedelic movies discussed in this book by Evan Mantri. And if I had been an ayahuasca tourist in Latin America, I would not be learning so much from Jack Lieberman's chapter about taking that shamanic preparation with his daughter in the Amazon. All this and more is told in just two sections of *Manifesting Minds*.

I suppose the heart of the book, for most skeptical readers, would be the sections on medicine and psychotherapy—MAPS bases one of its primary arguments on the ability of mindful molecules to help in healing. As early as the 1950s the world learned that some psychedelics could help free addicts from their dependency (for example, in Humphry Osmond's work in Canada), and more recently that MDMA could be useful as an adjunct to psychotherapy in treating PTSD. But so far, in the U.S., these modalities are available only in limited research studies.

However, the most far reaching part of this book is on how psychedelics can enhance the lives of the healthy—in breaking set patterns, in appreciating nature, in lovemaking, in social bonding, in the process of dying, in relating to the technological world that soon will surround us, and, as a research paper out of Johns Hopkins says, in occasioning "mystical-type experiences." More than a few writers make the point that the real reason for prohibition is not that taking mindful molecules (like many other activities) involve risks for some people, but rather that they are effective in leading many people outside consensus reality.

In the spirituality section, we are bombarded with more than we perhaps wish to know about the exact drugs, prescribed and not, taken by Tim Leary in his last days. But we also find Myron Stolaroff's chapter on learning how to learn, a set of instructions mainly about exploring through surrender or, less ambiguously, through letting go. "It is fresh, unmediated experience that we are seeking," he writes.

The book ends with an interview with Mark Pesce, who in addition to being an inventor is a futurist and entrepreneur. I don't know whether the computer industry, like western Buddhism, would have been as vigorous without its psychonauts, but apart from Nobel Prize winners such as Kary Mullis and some other notably creative people, we are unlikely to know the full story as long as mindful molecules are "scheduled" as being dangerous and without medical uses.

McKenna's conference in Kona was an effort to assert some of the positive uses of psychedelics, and perhaps to tempt more creative people to emerge from the ordinary-reality closet. *Manifesting Minds* continues and broadens this effort, including and then venturing far beyond the arts.

It is unclear whether a medical model offers the optimal alternative to the present protocol of illegality and very limited research, but a system based on prescriptions may be the most probable next step. To the credit of the editors, this book contains material that also goes well beyond the medical model.

For example, John Allen's account of the peyote dance ceremony held by the Huichole in Mexico raises the question of whether the careful and legal use of mindful molecules in the form of classic psychedelics should be restricted in the U.S. to so-called indigenous groups, such as the Native American Church and a small offshoot of a Brazilian church. Perhaps these substances should become available, in ritual settings, to other people too?

Allen's experience of attaining a deep ecological understanding through the structured use of peyote caused him to return to his central question: "Could this be achieved without peyote or equivalent real-time sacrament to raise the human organism to its capacity to make a workable synergy of reason, feeling, sensation, and will that coordinates its life with bioregion and cosmos? Frankly, I don't think so."

# Social Justice

# CHAPTER 19

# Welcoming Warriors Home

O ne of the dubious benefits of "voluntary" recruitment into the military, rather than a draft, is that presidents can more easily conduct wars despite a skeptical public, and another is that some civilians can regard military service as mainly another cash transaction, as if to say to PTSD sufferers "nobody forced them, too bad if they claim to be invisibly hurt."

Warriors throughout the ages have had a need to be welcomed home by their communities. Regardless of how we regard the wars in Afghanistan, Iraq, and earlier in Vietnam, what might be a decent way to help reintegrate soldiers who have served in our name?

One answer is shown in the astonishing film, *The Welcome*, produced by psychotherapist Bill McMillan and filmmaker Kim Shelton, a couple who also organized the events depicted in the film.[15]

Not about fighting abroad, but about telling the truth about it at home, and about listening to that truth, the film takes us inside a workshop for returning veterans led by Michael Meade, who has worked with Robert Bly and who is praised for his "hypnotic and fiery storytelling, street savvy perceptiveness, and spellbinding interpretations of ancient myths."

At the start of the workshop, held in a sylvan setting, many vets sat with arms crossed and looks of polite skepticism. In the course of several days together, they were led first to talking about their experience of war, then to writing truthful, heart-wrenching poems about it. After a bus ride into town, they shared some of these poems on Memorial Day in a packed 650-seat theater of the Oregon Shakespeare Festival in Ashland.

Reviewing the film, a critic for the state's biggest newspaper began by writing, "Sometimes you stumble into something out of a sense of duty or good intentions only to find yourself absorbed and overwhelmed beyond anything you might have anticipated." Judging by the sobs and gasps that I heard, the screening provided more than a minor catharsis for the audience; and as confirmed by the standing ovation in Ashland's historic armory, the film is brilliant in its intimacy, pacing, and novelty.

After the screening, ten or so of the people in the film took the stage for questions, including a mother who fought for the rehabilitation of her son who had been grievously wounded in an explosion.

Bill McMillan once explained, "For many vets coming back, they go from intensity and hypervigilance and clarity of purpose, which primarily means taking care of each other; they come back and the intensity isn't here, the focus isn't here. They often can't find jobs."

Ed Tick, clinical psychotherapist and author of *War and the Soul*, has taken part in healing vets since the Vietnam War. "Years later," he explains, "veterans still have nightmares and flashbacks in which the old battles still rage. They still watch for threats and stand poised for danger. Their hearts respond to everyday situations as though they were vicious attacks..." For a returning vet in his (and now her) mid-twenties, post-traumatic stress might last more than half a century.

To what extent can *The Welcome* help national and local organizations provide a model for workshops and ceremonies elsewhere for returning warriors? Inspiring community members to embrace and assist returning veterans is certainly an important outcome for many who have viewed the film.

In addition, two relevant organizations which offer vet-to-vet assistance, helping veterans and their families who are enduring a crisis or who have a critical need for help, are the National Veterans Foundation and a group called Iraq and Afghanistan Veterans of America.

# CHAPTER 20

# Martin Luther King's Legacy

The main talent of Martin Luther King Jr., among many, was an ability to lift into wide awareness brutality and unfairness that a majority had been willing to ignore. And while the struggle for racial justice is not over, MLK helped lead the way to notable success.

In his 1963 "Letter from Birmingham Jail," King responded to a challenge from white religious leaders who sought to dissuade him from disobeying the law and causing trouble; who urged him to "wait." In the margin of newspapers, the only paper available to him in that jail, King composed one of the greatest letters in U.S. history, which was eventually smuggled out by his lawyer. He methodically replied to objection after objection against his civil rights campaign, explaining his values that had originated in a religion long served by his family; and justifying his methods, inspired in part by Gandhi, who had been influenced by our homegrown Thoreau.

King is the only American, apart from our first president, who has a Federal holiday named after him. Is King mainly celebrated for his appeal to conscience, his nonviolence? People are flattered to be regarded as acting in accord with a conscience. With regard to race, Americans agree, at least in principle, that the system should be open to talent wherever it appears, that nobody should be discriminated against.

Every system has its ways of dealing with unwanted

information. Under Stalin the Soviets edited fallen figures out of photographs; in a free country we prefer the "bear hug," the embrace of a figure's least objectionable sides. Thus, King is recalled for his seventeen minute "I Have a Dream" speech given in 1963 with a huge marble Lincoln gazing over his shoulder, but we hear scant mention of his speech at Riverside Church in 1967.[16]

As reaction to the latter speech revealed, Americans might be willing to grant fair access to the system, even grant it to the offspring of slaves, but woe to anyone who raises questions about the type of system we have. King was invited to the Riverside Church by "Clergy and Laymen Concerned about Vietnam," an anti-war group. In a slow, eloquent voice, he gave reasons for opposing continuation of U.S. involvement in that war, and for favoring Federal action against poverty, which would require money otherwise spent on the military. "A nation that continues year after year to spend more money on military defense than on programs of social uplift is approaching spiritual death," he said.

Blistering criticism came from important publishers, even some who had supported Dr. King's racial struggle. *The Washington Post* wrote that King had "diminished his usefulness to his cause, his country, his people." *LIFE* magazine characterized the speech as "demagogic slander that sounded like a script for Radio Hanoi."

Today we face a different challenge, in the form of climate change, but we too have a majority of people who are seemingly ignoring a danger, as many were willing in King's era to ignore an injustice. And again, the challenge is to raise widespread awareness of the situation and the solutions.

Everybody knows—well, most people sort of know—that we have a problem, but it's imagined to be far off. And many people doubt we could get other countries to go along, or assume we could "adapt" to weird weather, while some hope that an unforeseen technical discovery or initiative will save us. Besides, it is alleged, without careful analysis, or any analysis at all, that an attempt to preserve the climate would wreck the economy. We don't want to pay more for energy or have less, and don't yet feel, as MLK once said, "the fierce urgency of now" which he impressed us within regard to the urgent need for civil rights

# CHAPTER 21

# John Monro's Mission

In contrast to the normal search for comfort and security, John U. Monro had a tropism toward challenge, tracking it the way a sunflower follows the brightest point in the sky. Leaving the deanship at Harvard College in 1967, Monro was famous for taking a humble job at Miles College, a black school in the south that had lost its accreditation and where he started a program for incoming freshmen, some of whom were reading at a seventh-grade level. Friends assumed he was making a sacrifice and was some kind of saint.

As a college kid who met Monro in his office, and later assisted him in teaching a freshman seminar, I believe he was seeking a challenge greater than deciding what hours women could be in Ivy League men's rooms. He'd done what he could do at Harvard, looking after the less affluent, veterans, public school graduates, commuters, Peace Corps volunteers, and extension students. He'd helped open Harvard to the big world of people who, unlike him, didn't come from an old colonial family, people who hadn't attended a prestigious prep school.

While parts of JUM's exemplary story have long been known to friends, they were all lovingly gathered and put together into a biography called *John U. Monro: Uncommon Educator* by Toni-Lee Capossela, published by the Louisiana State University Press. Why a southern publisher? Because Monro sought a second career in the south, remaining there until he retired.

When I had the opportunity to work a bit with Monro I was a generation younger than he, and didn't know many of the details tenaciously discovered by the author of this well balanced, far-reaching biography, a book as uncommon as its subject. In addition to this excellent investigative work, the author avoided the traps of both hagiography and callow armchair criticism that mar many books about famous people.

The biography is absorbing because Monro is a model of moving deliberately out of one's comfort zone, instead of just dwelling there. The settings range, going back in time, from the deep south during the civil rights struggle, to Harvard Yard, to an aircraft carrier in the Pacific war, and to towns in eastern Massachusetts where young Monro grew up— commuting first to a neighboring town's school and then to Andover, a prep school mainly for boarders.

While the biography starts with ancestors, the most amazing early part describes Monro's years as wartime "damage control officer" aboard the aircraft carrier Enterprise. Without any duties until the ship was attacked, Monro, after a shell or kamikaze pilot hit, was suddenly one of the most important officers aboard. As the biography makes clear, his ingenuity and calm saved the ship on several occasions—for instance with a repair that enabled the Enterprise to fight on without making the long trip to a U.S. dry dock, if not to the bottom of the Pacific.

After the war Monro defined his job, in part, as winning access to Harvard for unconventional students, helping to convert that Ivy League college from serving largely as a finishing school for sons of privilege to being an arena of opportunity for talent that was prepared for it. Most of the kids who attended had never been exposed to poverty such as Peace Corps volunteers encountered in, for example, Nigeria; had no idea of the experience of black kids in the U.S., disadvantaged by inferior schools and locked out of most careers.

Monro admired clear, ingenious, capacious thinking, which for him was expressed, and often learned, through the enterprise of writing. When Harvard received funds for an experimental freshman seminar program, he volunteered to teach "expository" prose. As his teaching assistant, I watched as he challenged and supported kids whom he took the trouble to know personally.

In those years undergraduates called an easy course a "gut." Monro's seminar was no gut. It was challenging, but what he assumed and assured was that everybody would succeed. Like the students who were just a few years younger, I was pretending to have it all together, while actually my first experience of teaching was challenging. At whatever level the students were, Monro kept eliciting the next level of articulateness. We all had a long way to go.

But teaching privileged kids who'd been to good schools, knew how to take tests, and were poised to enter some kind of elite could not, like being a dean of students, challenge Monro forever. It was a glorious task to stretch financial aid to cover a maximum number of people who needed it, who were prepared to do the work and move gracefully into an Ivy League college, but what about talent that, by the age of eighteen, had been neglected? What about kids who hadn't been raised to regard themselves as "elite"?

Here is where somebody was needed to perform a kind of damage control on our society, which had a hole blown close to the waterline, a hole called slavery and its aftermath. Toward the end of WWII a book appeared from Swedish author Gunnar Myrdal entitled *An American Dilemma: The*

*Negro Problem and Modern Democracy.* The book's thesis was that the U.S. had admirable ideals, but was struggling to apply them to former slaves; and when measured against the values, the performance could be dismissed as hypocritical. But Myrdal also argued that the ideals were a great contribution to human welfare, and needed only to be taken more seriously.

When he was invited to apply for the presidency of a southern black college, Monro realized that black Americans had to enlarge their own leadership class. What he could do was help. The programs that he founded first at Miles, and then at Tougaloo in Mississippi, were each gradually absorbed into the departmental structure of the colleges, and in this sense, like many other Caucasians who took part in securing some rights for black Americans, Monro was eventually pushed aside—although less by black power in his case than by holders of advanced degrees.

Meanwhile, however, he helped teach a generation how to think more clearly and write with more articulate energy. In going where the need was great, he offered a model of enhancing life by meeting tough challenges.

# Economic Initiatives

## CHAPTER 22

# Space Wealth

A s the ongoing brouhaha about asteroid mining shows, visionaries may toil quietly until rich or famous people decide to enact an idea. Director James Cameron (*Avatar*) and the founders of Google, along with others, are setting out to bring back valuable metals from "near-Earth asteroids" with their firm, Planetary Resources. The name apparently implies not only that the resources are to be found *on* this planet, but also that they will be brought back *to* it.

What is involved in asteroid mining? The go-to source is a non-profit organization called Space Wealth, cofounded by William BC Crandall, who edited an early book on nanotechnology for MIT Press (1996) and has an MBA from California Polytechnic State University. The key paper on this topic, "Profitable Asteroid Mining: A Pragmatic Policy Goal?," was written by Crandall, who answers its stated question about the policy goal with a resounding "Yes!"

Asteroids seem far away, except when viewers of a Hollywood movie worry about one crashing into Earth, but many near-Earth asteroids are easier to go to than the moon—in fact, a Japanese craft has already brought back a sample of the surface of an asteroid called Itokawa. According to Crandall, some asteroids are rich in platinum-group metals. (In late 2016 platinum was selling for about $1000/ounce.)

One of the technologies necessary for asteroid mining

would be robotics, with obvious applications also on Earth. It is not inconceivable that new robotics patents may in themselves provide a substantial income.

In an era of uncertain support for space ventures, successful asteroid mining would keep alive and extend the skills necessary for eventual habitats in space. Crandall and others hope that profitable asteroid mining might open a path to a viable future off of the Earth. In the words of Stephen Hawking, "The human race shouldn't have all its eggs in one basket, or on one planet."

# CHAPTER 23

# Economic Inequality

O ver breakfast with a client who had a $90 million fortune, I asked a hypothetical question: Would it decrease your motivation as an entrepreneur if it were understood that each year people with big incomes would be celebrated and, as if at a potlatch, would give back to the community all but some small multiple of the average family income?" After a forkful of Spanish omelet he told me "No, it wouldn't decrease my motivation or my business creativity; what other game would I play?"

As my client knew, the potlatch, a Native American custom in the Northwest, was a feast at which prosperous members of the community sought prestige not by having wealth, but by giving it away.

Let's plug in figures for a conservative yield on my client's fortune and for the average family income. Even allowing no deductions at all, he would be giving away the equivalent of an income tax even higher than the 91 percent charged under Eisenhower for the biggest incomes.

The sample size of my breakfast survey was just one, and the respondent was unusual—as a philanthropist, he was already giving some of his fortune away and he had a broad worldview. He took seriously the claim that, above a certain level, money is only a way of keeping score.

I thought of his reply when reading the results of a survey of a representative sample of more than 5,000 U.S.

residents commissioned by a Michael I. Norton, professor at the Harvard Business School, and Dan Ariely, a colleague at Duke University. They found that the average U.S. citizen radically underestimates the actual U.S. inequality, and regards as ideal even less inequality than he or she mistakenly thinks now prevails. Here are the figures from their survey:

The sample regarded as fair was a 32 percent share of the national wealth for the top fifth of the population ("quintile").

What they thought was the actual share of this same group: 59 percent

The actual share at the time of the survey: 84 percent

The gaps here are so extreme as to raise the question: In a country proud of its democracy, how does the top fifth get away with owning 84 percent of the national wealth? Even more startling, how is the top 1 percent of people allowed to own nearly 50 percent of the wealth? Since Norton and Ariely's paper was published in 2011, the inequality has grown, so these gaps are even more staggering.

In the last thirty plus years, since around the start of the 1980s, we have witnessed, apart from the rich, only a "stagnation" of income. So far, this "plateau" has been disguised by more than one member of the household working, by the availability of cheap goods from abroad, and by the hidden tax of inflation (when dollar income rises, but purchasing power does not).

We could find many explanations for toleration of the present disparity, but they probably rely on the "little people" not suffering a noticeable decline in purchasing power. In other words, I suggest that the American Dream can tolerate shifting from "will be better off than the prior generation" (a rise) to "will be no worse off" (a plateau), but perhaps not to "will have notably less" (a fall).

After college my first job was teaching assistant in a course on "American Character and Social Structure" given by the social observer David Riesman, author of *The Lonely Crowd*. We examined the distinction between economic equality of result (claimed by our enemy of that time, the Soviet Union) and what this country allegedly had, or at least sought, which was "equality of opportunity."

Ambition, ingenuity, and hard work would be "rewarded" by whatever money could be extracted from "the free market." As much as possible, we were supposed to have a "level playing field," on which merit and energy would seek to score. People who did well "deserved" everything they got: why should they pay taxes for anything but the military and a few other essentials? Let everything else be "privatized."

According to Erin Currier of the Economic Mobility Project, "There is not equality of opportunity in the way we as a nation imagine there is." In her view, based on research, "the American Dream is struggling."

The Motion Picture Academy gave an Oscar for best documentary to *Inside Job*, an expose of what its director, Charles Ferguson, regards as "systemic corruption" in the financial services industry. However, while most Americans still don't want to inquire too deeply into the financial system (any more than they want to draw conclusions from scientific findings about climate change or the peak of traditional petroleum production), we continue to barrel ahead despite the prospect of declining global production of traditional oil, a growing demand for it, and evidence that the price of oil above a certain amount leads to severe recession. (Although at the time of publication, a global oil glut due to fracking and use of tar sands fields appeared as if it would continue to keep prices low at least for the short term.)

Revolts in so-called developing countries can be predicted not only by the fraction of educated youth who are unemployed (as well as other factors), but also by the fraction of household budgets spent for food. Now we might ask of developed countries: To what extent will voters tolerate extreme inequality if the standard of living of a large majority of them no longer gradually rises, or at least seems to remain stable, but actually declines noticeably? The political response to this situation may not be rational.

# CHAPTER 24

# The Freedom of Simple Living

Every Saturday my Dad would sit down with a tall book that said "Ledger" on the front and enter into it all checks written and receipts saved by his wife. (Today we do it on a screen.) The tense exercise would always end with Dad being annoyed, if not angry, then calling his wife in and informing her that she had spent all the money they had. Mom would then proceed to tell him proudly about all the bargains she had found and just couldn't resist. And did he want to shortchange the kids?

I was about twelve when I realized that if just five percent less were spent, every Saturday would be an occasion of joy. Would the family have been deprived? On the salary of an engineer, who was also vice president of a small manufacturing company, we had a leafy back yard, a dishwasher, and an early TV. There was no reason my parents couldn't save even ten percent, and spend a moment of their weekends envisioning all the treats this would some day make possible.

Given the levels of prosperity in the U.S. at that time, we could have been happy at any level above poverty, except for one thing—newspapers, magazines, billboards, shop windows, radio, and TV were all carrying ads for stuff to buy. If the civic religion of the country had a short motto it would have been progress; defined more precisely as economic growth. If we were ever tempted to moderate our relentless consumerism, we had friends against whom it was natural to measure our success. We could not afford to "fall behind," to "lower our standard of living."

It did not help that my mother's dad, the happiest man I knew, was living on much less. This beloved grandfather of mine, who used to take me fishing in a small boat we'd had the pleasure of building together, could easily have told me the story of the Mexican fisherman that I heard years later from a California entrepreneur:

A gringo hires a boat in Cabo San Lucas and gets friendly with the captain. Over the bait pail, he advises the Mexican to take out a loan to acquire another boat, hire a crew to run it, and build up a big fishing business. When the captain asks where this would lead, the gringo says that the Mexican could eventually make a million (dollars, not pesos). "And what then?" asks the captain. After a moment they both laugh, the obvious answer being he'd retire and go fishing.

When the purchasing power of the middle class began to fall, we in the U.S. compensated by (a) women going to work, (b) buying cheap stuff made by folks abroad who were given jobs that had once been American, and (c) taking out loans on our plastic. One household in ten even rents a storage unit for stuff that won't fit in the attic or garage. What we did not do is buy less.

As Joe Dominguez and Vicki Robin showed in their book *Your Money or Your Life*, the dollars used to buy this stuff do not come free—they cost the part of our lives that we spend working for the necessary income. Many workers do not enjoy their jobs, but they have bills to pay and, in effect, they become indentured servants to a system that promises happiness but delivers mainly "stuff." The stuff brings only brief pleasure, which then fades; then it's time to buy something more.

It is contrary to commercial and financial interests to talk of living on less rather than more. In fact, we are taught that progress *means* getting more. But this definition of success is the bait on the hook. If you think the system through, we even pay to be taught to consume because the cost of advertising is folded into the price of the product.

A minority has long doubted the merits of this system. For example, Thoreau said that real wealth is "knowing how much you can do without."[17] Some people are famous for living simply, as Helen and Scott Nearing did; and every so often somebody writes about the joy of "voluntary simplicity," as Duane Elgin did in 1981 at the start of the Reagan era. Today there are relevant websites like "simpleliving.net" and "bemorewithless.com," but living on less than one earns is relentlessly countered by pervasive advertising which is reinforced by peers who are also subjected to, and influenced by, these same ads.

After watching the results of this program of infinite growth on a finite planet, Herman Daly, former chief economist of the World Bank, wrote in favor of what he calls a "steady-state economy."

There is something we as individuals can do: People who feel powerless to alter official policy about climate change can nonetheless decide how much of their personal income to spend. What would happen if even a substantial fraction decided to find value in something other than stuff?

One objection to simple living is that the economy would shrink if everybody adopted this practice. Perhaps you could reframe that argument as an observation that people would not spend as much of their lives earning money to buy stuff they don't really need. We'd have less stuff, but more time.

Simple living produces much lower stress and less need for anti-anxiety medicines while leading to a feeling of freedom that is not dependent on income level. I've known rich people who feel inferior to friends who are even richer. The key is to spend less than we earn, growing other values and just ignoring (or laughing at) all the blandishments of an economic system dependent on our craving every last thing we can get.

# CHAPTER 25

# Back to the Farm

*This interview with Chris Jagger, a young organic farmer from Blue Fox Farm in the Applegate Valley of Southern Oregon, took place in December of 2014.*

**CKC: How did you decide to go into growing food?**

**CJ:** When I was in college, and eating largely from the fast food chains, I started to become interested in sourcing the food I was eating. At some point I had a shift and started looking for something more nutritious. Then, when I began working in a co-op in the Midwest, I asked: "Where does all this food come from that we sell at the co-op?" When I moved out to the West Coast it happened that my now-wife was studying agroecology at Santa Cruz, and it all just clicked in at that point.

**CKC: Trace out the path from when you made the decision to become a farmer; what did you do next?**

**CJ:** I grew up in Missouri and was surrounded by farms, though a different style of farm from what we have here—it was a world of corn, beans, and cattle. So I had that in my roots; and my family had been farmers in the past. Once I knew that was the direction I wanted to head in, it all started to come back. My now-wife and I just started to work on farms in the Santa Cruz area as laborers, and figured if we could pick tomatoes for ten hours a day, and come back the next day, we must really enjoy it. Later we interned on separate farms in Colorado, as well as managing the vegetable part of a farm there—that's where we started to hone our skills at really running a farm. Then we moved to Oregon.

**CKC: How did you get your farm here in the Rogue Valley?**

**CJ:** We had no intention of coming out here, and were actually on the way to buy a farm near Cortez, Colorado. But it got sold out from underneath us. In hindsight, that was the right thing. The very next day, my wife's father was looking for an area to retire in, and my wife and I had been through this area on our travels up and down the West Coast. Liking it here, we started investigating online. This was about the time that Google was starting so we used the search engine.

**CKC: I should add here that you have a blog, in fact two blogs. This is not our image of the traditional farmer.**

**CJ:** No, it's the twenty-first century farmer.

**CKC: So is the farm a family enterprise?**

**CJ:** We first helped a friend at a dairy he was starting while we were looking for land. My wife's sister and her husband expressed interest in coming up from the San Diego area and joining us in the farming venture, then the sisters' parents decided they would like to be part of the venture, too. So we bought the farm collectively as a family, and the two couples operate the farm while the parents live in a nearby town.

**CKC: What other models of acquiring land to grow food do you find in people around you?**

**CJ:** A lot of people look into leasing plans, especially if they can't afford a down payment. Fortunately, in our case, as a family we had enough collective buying power. Other folks had an inheritance that they used to buy land. For people who do not have a family unit that can make a down payment, leasing is probably the best way to start. Now that we have been in the area for some years we are offered pieces of land, quite often actually, but there is only so much we can do.

**CKC: Given that it rarely rains here during the growing season, how do you get water?**

**CJ:** Our water comes from Williams Creek and the Applegate River. The creek through our main farm goes dry every year, so before we built a pond that was part of the reason we looked into leasing other land. In the Midwest or back East, it's a completely different ballgame.

**CKC: If local food growing is going to be ramped up, what can help people get land and whatever else they need?**

**CJ:** Land preservation is the key. If we see all the good farming land in this area go for development, as some of the best land already has ... I'm all for housing, but we have to learn to build on the less fertile soil, and preserve the rest to be grown on. There are several pieces in this area with premier class-one soils that are for sale. A wise community would find a way of acquiring that land and setting it aside in a trust for food growing, and find the people to work it.

**CKC: What about a person who owns land and hopes to make a lot of money on it, perhaps in order to retire? In this situation, how does land get preserved for agriculture use?**

**CJ:** Usually by the owner talking with a land trust, such as the Southern Oregon Land Conservancy. A lot of these types of organizations buy up the development rights, which helps curtail the costs to the farmer, who then only has to pay for agricultural rights.

**CKC: Where do the land trusts get the money to do this?**

**CJ:** Through fundraising. A community could come together and decide this is something they want to do, whether it's Ashland as a city or the Rogue Valley as a region. Food security is an issue we really need to look at.

**CKC: One model is the village farm, like we have here in Ashland, based on leasing land and farming it cooperatively, where the people who give their labor get the food. How do you distribute the food that you grow?**

**CJ:** We sell at the farmers markets in Ashland and Grants Pass, the co-op in Ashland, and we have several restaurant accounts. We used to do a classic CSA (community supported agriculture) box system, but have adapted this to a hybrid system using "market bucks." Instead of getting a box of assorted vegetables each week in the classic way, people come to market and shop for exactly what they want if they have a membership with us.

**CKC: This is a coupon system?**

**CJ:** Definitely. This came out of necessity for us because we have a young boy and wanted to spend more time with him in the evenings on harvest days, so we needed to cut down on the time we were spending packing boxes. Plus about 80 percent of our membership was picking up at market anyway, getting their boxes of assorted vegetables, then coming around to the front and buying additional produce. So we said, "Let's give people the choice." And those who travel in the summer and don't need a box when they're away can just use the service when they do need it.

**CKC: The "market bucks" are sold at a discount?**

**CJ:** They are. People pay upfront for the membership, which gives farmers starting capital so we don't have to take out loans. A full membership is $500, but it's discounted to $425. And we keep in touch with the buyers via our blog each week telling what we are going to have at market, and what's going on at the farm as well. For us, the Internet is just another farming tool, like a spading machine or a tiller. I wanted to keep up with the coming generation, to communicate with them. Fifteen or twenty years from now I hope to still be doing that.

**CKC: You mention equipment, and I understand you have an electric tractor. Why?**

**CJ:** It's a converted 1949 Allis Chalmers "G" model. We converted it from gasoline to electric. I am mechanically minded, I like tinkering; just the idea of getting away from the gas engine really appealed to me, moving in the direction of trying to be more sustainable. I don't know if any farm will ever be fully sustainable, but we have to head down that path.

**CKC: What about skilled labor, where do you find the necessary people?**

**CJ:** We've hired day laborers, and brought apprentices onto the farm to teach them what we know. We have been as diverse with our labor pool as with what we are growing on the farm. In the first years all our labor came from my wife and me, with no outside labor except for a friend who occasionally came up.

**CKC: A few years ago my wife and I came over a rise and saw your leased land full of vegetables, and one of us said, "This is real wealth." The field was too big to have been worked only by you and your wife.**

**CJ:** After the first years, a lot of people have come out—friends, volunteers, apprentices. Family has played a big part, too.

**CKC: What is the offer that you'll make to a potential apprentice?**

**CJ:** Usually we require a certain number of days per week, and there's a lot of information exchange that goes on throughout the whole week. We give them housing, and they get board as well—they're not just coming for a job, they are living an experience. Most people who come to apprentice with us are people who want to go on to become farmers. It worked for us, so we're hoping to pass the knowledge along.

**CKC: Why are young people attracted to the farming lifestyle?**

**CJ:** I think it feels real. People are looking for their roots. That's what it was for me. I wanted to find out where it all came from, the earth. A lot of people want to get back to that starting place even if they do not consciously know it.

**CKC: Do you think we can fund farms so land can be bought for young farmers?**

**CJ:** In the East, and now also in California, there is an interesting model called Farm Link. It's basically older farmers saying, "I have a piece of land to be farmed," and the organization then links them to young people who want to farm. For example, I have a friend in Santa Cruz who has been linked to a 65-year-old farmer in the Monterey area with established orchards and vineyards.

CHAPTER 26

# Tilling Our Own Soil

W hat percentage of the food eaten in the Rogue Valley is grown here?" I asked a young Oregon farmer while handing him a $500 check one spring for a season's worth of weekly produce filling boxes big enough to feed four people. When you sign up for Community Supported Agriculture (CSA), or graze tables covered with produce at a growers market, it's easy to overestimate how much food is grown locally, but the farmer's reply startled me. "The figure could be as high as high as one percent" he replied after a pause.

The number of individuals and families participating in CSA programs is small, but it is increasing. In 2002, for example, Fry Family Farm in Talent supplied 95 weekly CSA boxes; in 2016 they supplied around 150 boxes. Given that the population of Jackson County is currently just above 200,000 people, the numbers are still a fraction of what they could be. Of course farmers in our region also sell at open-air markets and roadside stands, as well as to local restaurants and those grocery stores willing to stock locally grown produce. But with regard to the percentage of food eaten in the valley that's grown here, whatever the exact percentage is, the figure is still tiny.

The system of getting nearly all of our food from industrial agriculture located elsewhere works as long as petrochemicals are cheap, as they have been (with brief interruptions) for many decades. Natural gas fuels some of the electricity used for refrigeration and plays an integral role in the manufacture of nitrogen fertilizer, using a process invented in 1908 by German chemist and Nobel Laureate Fritz Haber. Just a century ago, farmers depended mainly on nitrogen-fixing cover crops, manure, and bird guano for fertilizer. Crude oil also serves as the feedstock for pesticides and herbicides, for packaging, and as fuel for farm equipment and long-distance trucks. Without cheap petrochemicals, the system of industrial agriculture would falter.

Why should this worry us? Perhaps because although U.S. oil production, which had been declining since around 1970, had a temporary boom between 2010 and 2016, productivity associated with this increase showed a continued decrease at the end of 2016; the main foreign sources are in politically volatile areas; and some suppliers claim dubious reserves. Matt Simmons is a veteran oil industry analyst who, after examining 200 technical papers, published a book on OPEC's biggest single supplier under the title *Twilight in the Desert: The Coming Saudi Oil Shock and the World Economy* (Wiley & Sons, 2005), in which he argues that the Saudis, like others, have exaggerated the size of their reserves.

If the world soon reaches the "peak" of traditional petroleum (and later of natural gas) production, the price of food will increase. While we wouldn't be out of petrochemicals, we would be dependent on oil that is harder to find and bring to the surface, and thus more costly. With regard to food, the economic advantage would tip back toward harvesting from fields closer to consumers, and toward growing produce by organic methods with as little dependence as possible on gas and oil.

How ready are we for this scenario? Short answer: We're not ready now, but the transition could be accomplished, especially if we start preparing. The percentage of food produced locally would have to rise from one to closer to one hundred, which can be done not only by an expansion of local farming but also by a rapid growth in urban horticulture. During both world wars, the U.S. Department of Agriculture sponsored a social invention called "victory gardens," with twenty million Americans responding to the call to grow their own food. Gardens in yards, vacant lots, and parks supplied up to 40 percent of the produce eaten throughout the war years. (My own earliest memory is of crawling under tomato plants in a wartime garden.)

When the U.S.S.R. was about to collapse in the late 1980s, some became concerned that its collective agriculture might soon do an even worse job than it had already done in providing food to its citizens. A project in decentralized urban farming was begun, and on all-Soviet television a foreign visitor from a non-governmental organization made the point that in order to get vegetables you don't have to wait for a government bureaucracy—you can dig the soil (even next to a housing project), plant seeds, and then water the row.

After the collapse of the Soviet Union, Russia was no longer able to subsidize Cuban sugar by sending cheap oil and agricultural chemicals. Out of necessity, the Castro regime supported extensive organic truck farming and urban horticulture in the city of Havana and other urban areas. During the so-called "special period," Cubans got more exercise, ate fresher food, and lost an average of twenty pounds each.

In the U.S., it is hard to imagine having to pay a much larger fraction of our income for food, not to mention facing shortages like those faced by the Soviets and the Cubans. But the supply of foreign oil is uncertain, and competition for it is growing as the Chinese and Indian markets join the West in demanding more. Alternatives are problematic. Nuclear power takes a long time to build, and nobody has figured out how to effectively and safely handle the radioactive waste. Coal contributes heavily to global climate change and air pollution. Wind power and solar panels are less energy intensive than oil but, like nuclear and coal, can't fuel our present vehicle fleet. Coal liquefaction is environmentally challenging. Ethanol from corn, according to some studies, takes about as much energy to produce as it yields. It also removes some food from the market.

In other words, even setting aside all the other effects of more expensive oil, it's worth imagining how we might adapt to a future with much higher food costs. So far, it is the Pentagon that has done much of the "contingency planning" in our society. Most of these plans are never used, but a few do turn out to be crucial. In a similar spirit, can we civilians plan for events that may never happen, but that would be much worse unless we know what to do and start preparing for them?

Hospitals build in a "surge capacity," defined by the Agency for Healthcare Research and Quality as "a health care system's ability to rapidly expand beyond normal services to meet the increased demand for qualified personnel, medical care, and public health." Meaning they can handle many more patients in an emergency than in normal times, a capacity needed if there is an epidemic, large accident, or other disaster. In terms of a potential shortage of an affordable and healthy food supply, can we also design a surge capacity?

Thanks to English horticulturist Alan Chadwick, attaining a surge capacity for food may be less difficult than it once was. In the 1960s, Chadwick went to Santa Cruz, California and created a large vegetable garden, pioneering what was called "bio-intensive" horticulture. His students and colleagues have fanned out over the intervening years, some of them to the State of Jefferson (southwestern Oregon and far northern California). The best known is John Jeavons, author of *How to Grow More Vegetables: And Fruits, Nuts, Berries, Grains, and Other Crops Than You Ever Thought Possible on Less Land Than You Can Imagine* (Ten Speed Press, 2006), now in its 7th edition. Jeavons lives and teaches in Willits, California and says depending on local climate, soil quality, and the skill of the grower, a bio-intensive garden as small as 800 square feet (just 20' x 40') can provide a family of four with fresh vegetables year round.

Another person whose life was touched by Chadwick's garden is Scott (Hawkeye) McGuire, who attended college in Santa Cruz and now works as a landscaper in the Rogue Valley while maintaining a large produce garden. "I've heard that during the Great Depression 90 percent of Americans had some relative living on a family farm," he explains. "Today it's down to a handful." Anticipating the time when we will need to grow more of what we eat, McGuire offers workshops on horticulture, and observes that it is much easier to enlarge an existing garden than start one from scratch. Among the many factors of food production, McGuire starts with the seeds and recommends developing viable seed bank networks. Our success in growing more of our own food, he says, will depend on the length of transition we experience. A garden takes time to establish, even if you start in the early spring.

John Fisher-Smith, an Ashland resident, author, Jefferson Public Radio commentator, and former architect has established at least eight large vegetable gardens. After spending his adolescence on an organic farm in Bucks

County, Pennsylvania, Fisher-Smith also learned from the bio-intensive methods developed by Allen Chadwick and, when his oldest son decided he wanted to learn vegetable gardening, took him to meet John Jeavons. Through the years, Fisher-Smith did more than his share of "double-digging" and intensive soil building, but in his eighties has become what he calls a "lazy gardener" who uses a rototiller and grows "the easy stuff" such as "corn, peas, asparagus, raspberries, winter squash, peppers, eggplant, carrots, leeks, garlic, and sweet onions." Fisher-Smith would not quarrel with my CSA supplier's estimate that our area now grows only one per cent of the food we eat locally. Nor would he be surprised if food becomes "very expensive."

Fortunately, growing food doesn't require a factory to be built, or rails to be laid. It requires sun, soil, and water, all of which we have here in the State of Jefferson. We also need good seeds (which can be harvested), along with simple tools, protective fencing, and a set of skills. To preserve the harvest we would need canning equipment and dehydrators, as well as cold storage.

So if we take this possibility of expensive food seriously, what is to be done? First of all, we would need an inventory of local people who can teach horticulture, a group that includes "master gardeners" and other experienced growers; with classes organized by civic groups, religious organizations, schools and colleges.

We would certainly be better prepared if our cities and towns inventoried land not being used for other purposes. During WWII, England passed a law that any idle land could be employed for growing food without compensation to the owners. Gardens sprang up, there as here, in yards around houses, yes, but also in vacant lots, "undeveloped" properties, parks, and other city land. Just as the U.S. gave away farm land in the nineteenth century to those who would work it, so too could land that sits idle be made available under fair and practical terms.

There may be a role for government and nonprofit entities alike in stockpiling seeds, watering devices, simple tools, and fencing for gardens. Ashland, for example, has a volunteer emergency service called CERT (Community Emergency Response Team), which could enlarge its range to deal not only with floods, earthquakes, and chemical spills, but also a possible shortage of affordable food.

Under the leadership of Alice Waters, founder of the renowned Bay Area restaurant Chez Panisse in Berkeley, California, public schools began a program of gardening, yielding produce then served in the cafeterias. As part of the educational program, this "edible schoolyard" introduces children to the skills of food growing and the delights of eating, as Waters would say, "fresh, according to the seasons," not primarily out of government surplus warehouses.

Obviously, if transportation became much more expensive, grocery stores that rely on distant suppliers would have no choice but to seek more local providers. In communities sponsoring extensive horticulture, some food would be taken directly from garden to table, but stores would still have a major role, as locally grown crops could be sold to local retailers for resale to the public. There would also be a need for preservation, such as canning, pickling, and dehydrating, which could be done in association with stores for foods to be sold throughout the colder, non-growing seasons. There are also many ways to grow edible crops year round, with and without greenhouses.

Food needs could be met not only by developing small-scale horticulture in and near towns, but also by enlarging the local agricultural sector. What would it take to induce more existing growers to enlarge their production, and to help more people begin? Clearly, land that is priced with an eye on "development" rather than agriculture would rule out many young prospective farmers. What provisions should society make now to get more of that land into local food production?

Chris Jagger, who with his wife Melanie Kuegler owns Blue Fox Farm in the Applegate Valley (Chapter 25), commended a program in California for "incubating" farmers by giving them a small plot to work as they learn the necessary skills. After the skills are learned, they need to acquire suitable land, and Jagger describes himself as "a total advocate of agro-squatting"—by which he means society should find a way to get idle land under cultivation through longterm and low-rent leasing, or by other appropriate means.

With the help of relatives, Jagger and his wife were able to buy much of the land they now cultivate. Knowing that most young people can't possibly buy local land for farming, he notes the "hordes of lots" that are potentially available locally for leasing. Melissa Mathewson, Oregon State University Small Farms Extension Agent for Douglas, Jackson, and Josephine counties (in the southwest of the state), has a database of people who own land they aren't using along with names of farmers who are seeking land. Jagger leases some land himself, and when showing the crop-filled acres to a visitor said he feels "like someone between a king and a peasant."

Small-scale horticulture takes time to get started; in this climate many crops can be harvested only once a year, and seeds must be started in the spring. Farming takes even longer in that land has to be found, acquired, fenced, and prepared. The commitment is even larger, may involve moving, and more than likely accruing some debt along with bigger equipment than a shovel and hose.

Are we satisfied with a system that so far provides for only a tiny percentage of our food to be grown locally? Think of acquiring a surge capacity for food as a form of insurance: What are we willing to invest in order to have a less perilous supply?

With regard to many other developments, our society has typically waited until challenges are undeniable before acting. But more and more situations seem to be emerging in which, if we wait until they are obvious to everyone, we will have waited too long. Will you have a part in preparing a surge capacity for local food?

# World Politics

# CHAPTER 27

# How Change Happened

When discussing basic social change we want to know what the habits of empire are, what kind of stories its leaders tell, what manner of effort is required to oppose the smooth lies told by power, what attitudes support this effort, what kind of opposition is likely, what time scale is probable. These, it seems to me, are some of the main topics that Adam Hochschild addresses in his engaging and wonderful series of histories.

In just a few of his books Hochschild has examined the scandal of the colonial Congo (*King Leopold's Ghost*, 1998); the anti-slavery movement in Great Britain (*Bury the Chains*, 2005); the fighting of, and opposition to, what we now call WWI (*To End All Wars*, 2011); and the Spanish Civil War's idealism and failure of its honorable cause (*Spain in Our Hearts: Americans in the Spanish Civil War*, 2016). Earlier, he wrote about South Africa and about Stalinism, as well as an account of growing up in his wealthy and powerful father's domestic world (*Half the Way Home*, 1986).

Three of Hochschild's books have been set largely in England and are stories of suffering, persistence, and in some cases, triumph. They are also illustrations of Margaret Mead's well-known observation that the great changes are all the work of initially small groups of people who often feel powerless. Unfortunately, this does not mean that if you are powerless you will succeed, but it does mean that even if you are tempted to feel hopeless you can press on knowing that most "overnight success" comes from persistence in the face of scorn and oppression.

Hochschild has heroes in each of these books: In the fight about the Congo, it's primarily E.D. Morel; in the anti-slavery movement, Thomas Clarkson; in the anti-war movement early in the prior century, Charlotte Despard plus Sylvia Pankhurst. Haven't heard of them? They deeply changed our world, and their work suggests lessons for our time. In Hochschild's lambent telling, one thing that stands out is how hard they worked and how insistently. They took risks. In many cases, they went to prison.

One character that keeps popping into Hochschild's ironically titled *To End All Wars* is the young Bertrand Russell. Apart from all the reasons many of us have to be grateful to Russell, I am personally thankful to him for giving me a peripatetic interview as we left an anti-war rally in Trafalgar Square, and preventing me, physically, from stepping off a curb in front of an omnibus as I was walking backward. Articulate, impassioned, he was also amused at the eagerness of a young American. And, I am happy to recall, at the age of sixty-nine he still had a firm grip!

Now that we are relatively advanced, it's hard to imagine a time when slavery was normal, or a colonial enterprise such as King Leopold's Congo, or trench warfare. Part of what Hochschild's characters did was to reveal—as investigative journalists and good historians also do—what was going on behind the denial and the false reassurances; and many pages of his books are devoted to the ghastly conditions and dangers that called forth the protests.

A 1983 TV movie called *The Day After* was set in the area of Lawrence, Kansas at a time when a fictional Berlin crisis escalated into an intercontinental nuclear exchange.

The missiles flew just before halfway into the movie, leaving time to witness the aftermath: not a limited disaster such as a tornado might cause, but electromagnetic pulses bringing failure in all electric devices, blasts that swallowed cities, and radioactive fallout over fields, houses, people.

For many in the huge ABC audience, this made-for-TV flick was probably the first time they vividly imagined how, in the words of the immortal bumper sticker, "A nuclear war can ruin your whole day." Four months later Mikhail Gorbachev came to power in Moscow, and in 1985 he and Ronald Reagan declared in Geneva that a nuclear war could not be won and must never be fought—quite a change of tone from the president's early years in the White House. Did the TV dramatization of what nuclear war would mean in the U.S. heartland play a role?

In the case of the Congo and the slave ships, not many people knew what was going on. It took a few who saw, told, and kept telling until finally they demanded some simple but enormous changes. In the case of industrial war, as we know, it did not stop after 1919. The anti-war activists were let out of prison, and some of them managed distinguished careers, while others faded away or emigrated. Then came WWII and all the smaller wars of the last century, including a few in which the West is currently engaged. But the anti-war people early in the twentieth century did make a point of conscience, a point that keeps nagging at the dominant mode.

A founder of *Mother Jones* magazine, Hochschild is socially engaged, as many great historians have been, such as Eric Hobsbawn, E.P. Thompson, and Howard Zinn on the left. In *To End All Wars*, he respects the complexity of the past, such as the splits within families: Sir John French was commander in chief on the western front, and later Viceroy of Ireland, while his sister, Charlotte Despard, was a pacifist, communist, and supporter of the Irish Republican Army. In the Pankhurst family of British suffragettes, to give another example, Sylvia was strongly antiwar, while her mother Emmeline was a defender of the state.

For a general reader, Hochschild gives as stirring an account as anyone of the descent into a conflict the cavalry would have called war, but which amounted to the slaughter of men living in sodden trenches and going "over the top" into machine gun fire. More important, he shows how the working of conscience can bring about, or begin to bring about, a systemic change. Historians may seem far from affecting current events, although President Kennedy had reportedly read Barbara Tuchman's *The Guns of August* before the Cuban missile crisis. Who knows what might have happened if he hadn't?

# CHAPTER 28

# Citizen Diplomacy

In *The Power of Impossible Ideas,* Sharon Tennison tells one of the great hidden stories of our age as she describes how her organization, now called the Center for Citizen Initiatives, helped to end the Cold War and build a better Russia. Included in this account are the many "ordinary" people who helped to invent and engage in citizen diplomacy during the early 1980s.

Although the U.S.S.R. ultimately collapsed in 1991, and the four decades before that included regional wars, space exploration, and an economic boom, the consequential events of that period also included something that nearly happened, more than once, but didn't, and something that seemed impossibly naïve but wasn't—and the two were closely related.

What nearly happened but didn't quite was a nuclear exchange in the northern hemisphere, missiles soaring over the Arctic sea ice that is now melting. In the fall of 1962, for example, the Cuban missile crisis unfolded over the famous thirteen days, and is remembered as a moment of American triumph. As Dean Rusk, the Secretary of State said, "We're eyeball to eyeball and I think the other fellow just blinked." But as his colleague, Secretary of Defense Robert McNamara, pointed out in a documentary film, holding his thumb and index finger barely apart, "We came this close" to nuclear war. That film, *The Fog of War,* was released forty years after those events; long after McNamara had found out about a nuclear secret that nobody in the U.S. knew at the time.

What's the status of something that didn't happen? Less than a year later, on September 26, 1963, alarms sounded in the Soviet control center for satellite detection of a nuclear missile launch, warning of a possible American first strike. The officer in charge, Stanlislav Petrov, couldn't believe something so terrible was happening and so he disobeyed orders: After immediately notifying superiors, he paused for five long minutes until radar stations could have observed incoming missiles, but didn't. What seemed like an attack was later reinterpreted as sunlight glinting off the cloud cover over Montana. Petrov disobeyed orders and his only consolation, apart from preventing a mistaken war, was a UN medal quietly awarded.

This situation persisted for the next twenty years. We don't know how many close calls happened (in *The Fog of War* McNamara reported three during his tenure), but others are probably hidden behind the veil of national security. A single close call would have been too many, when the penalty was what became known as "nuclear winter," a period when crops wouldn't grow. But how to undo the situation, managed by elites on both sides, each citing quite persuasively the danger of the other?

One contribution to extracting us from this dynamic was an American initiative called "citizen diplomacy," unexpectedly initiated in part by Sharon Tennison who, like most of us, was an ordinary person—in her case a Texas girl who grew up to become a nurse in San Francisco. When a physician at her hospital invited her to join Physicians for Social Responsibility and give local talks about the Cold War, she realized she didn't know much about the nuclear standoff, or about the enemy.

It was in a friend's kitchen that she heard a voice in her head saying one simple sentence, a message that changed her life: "It's time to go see the enemy." The Soviets gave her a visa, and said it would be okay for her to meet ordinary people if she were accompanied by one of their Intourist guides. Some of her friends agreed to join her.

The attitude of our national security elite, including the FBI, was doubtful, not to say hostile. Who were these innocent women and men who might just get in the way of proper diplomacy, be seduced by the Soviets, perhaps cause some sort of incident? Almost nobody thought that the Cold War would ever end, but Tennison's hopeful group went to Moscow and talked with strangers, ordinary people on the street, in parks, in the elegant subway, in humble apartments.

Tennison later worked on relations between her country and the U.S.S.R., and then Russia, for about a quarter century. She organized many programs, starting with the first Alcoholics Anonymous meeting in Russia and a large exchange program bringing more than 400 ordinary Soviets to the U.S. and arranging for them to "meet Middle America."

When Russians were finally allowed to start small businesses, but didn't know how, Tennison's organization brought many to the U.S. so they could observe the sort of business they wanted to start, and then helped them to network with and support each other back home.

She stayed on the job through the terrible 1990s when the Russian economy fell apart. She then worked with a large State Department grant to train entrepreneurs and with Rotary International to foster a civic culture of volunteer service in a society marked by pervasive lack of trust. She supported a campaign against the corruption that in the 1990s took the form of "mafias" that ran protection rackets, to be followed in the 2000s by bureaucrats who impeded businesses by demanding bribes.

Meanwhile, Tennison kept Congress in touch with her activities, by arranging meetings in both Russia and Washington. As she reminds us, President Eisenhower who agreed: "When the people lead, the leaders will follow."

Her book lets us in on one of the big untold stories of the late twentieth century, and citizen diplomacy in its many forms has implications for some of our present troubles. As she writes, "The world desperately needs citizen diplomacy to the Middle East and other trouble spots around the globe."

The situation in the U.S.S.R. was especially suited to citizen diplomacy. After years of propaganda on both sides, simple hospitality, and a glimpse of simple reality, was almost revolutionary. The U.S.S.R. was physically safe, and friendly Americans had a certain access to the mass media. All you had to say, as I had occasion to do on all-Soviet TV, was (1) some Americans were neither Cold Warriors nor what Lenin called "useful idiots" (followers of the Party line; (2) we wished a better life for people there; (3) what had the Cold War accomplished in four decades other than to endanger the world?

If Mikhail Gorbachev had not undertaken to change the faltering Soviet system, employing the centralized power of the General Secretary, the Cold War would not have ended as it did; Eastern Europe would not have been liberated; and we would not have become rivals and trading partners rather than enemies. If Gorbachev had not seen some new thinking in the West, would he have dared to normalize external relations? As it was, he met enormous and understandable suspicion on the government level. Was the Kremlin really changing, or was it all a trick, a "peace offensive" to throw us off our guard?

As Tennison tells in her book, I played a small part in

arranging some early support for her activities, and together, at a brunch, we discussed the elements of what became "Soviets, Meet Middle America." I saw my job at the Ark Foundation, which had been endowed by entrepreneur Don Carlson in the 1980s to help end the Cold War, as giving impossible challenges such that, as talented, passionate, persistent people worked to meet them, they might do something wonderful. I knew that bringing unofficial Soviet people to tour American cities was unprecedented, so we doubled down by specifying that they stay in private homes and meet school kids, attend backyard barbecues, talk on the radio, visit small businesses, be introduced by local officials, go to city council meetings, and attend religious services if they wanted to.

After years of having been told that Americans were greedy, exploitive demons, the Soviets went home reporting that their hearts had been touched by warm receptions. In short, rather than discussing arms control, the visitors entered the ordinary life of the other side.

Another book with the word "impossible" in the title is Vaclav Havel's memoir of going from prison to the presidency in Prague; yet another is by author Paul Rogat Loeb, who wrote *The Impossible Will Take A Little While*, a line borrowed from Billie Holiday. All of these writers were illustrating what it means to be a citizen, not just a "consumer." All faced tasks that looked daunting. When I first met with Tennison in 1987, I told her the Ark Foundation was looking for leaders who didn't assume that things that seemed impossible necessarily were, and who didn't wait for a grant to get started. She met both criteria.

While Carlson didn't know whether it would be possible to end the Cold War, he judged that if it couldn't be ended, nothing else would matter. For that reason, we focused on that single goal for five years, ending in 1989 with the breaching of the Berlin Wall.

Tennison, to her credit, didn't stop. As the U.S.S.R. collapsed, she kept going through the terrible 1990s, when most of the Western media perceived a flowering of democracy, and Russians saw "oligarchs" grabbing control of big industries, mafias running rampant, and people going hungry. At the time of this writing, in 2016, her mission of engaging with the Russian people continues.

In *The Power of Impossible Ideas*, a word that comes up many times is "trust"—as in "lack of trust." One consequence of living under Stalin was that the level of trust was very low: Who would not betray you? People kept their private lives hidden. One of the shocking parts of Tennison's book is her talk with Putin's economic adviser, who laughed at her innocent question about whom the President, in a nearby Kremlin office, could trust. "Almost nobody," was the answer.

To Tennison's annoyance and alarm, much Western reporting took the side of the oligarchs—some of whom Putin was arresting. Maybe they did take possession of huge enterprises in the 1990s, but in the West they were familiar kinds of figures, like captains of industry; and at least they weren't commissars. And Putin, though perhaps honest, had come up through the KGB and was acting like a czar, at least as compared with his predecessor Yeltsin who, when not drunk, won approval in the West by praising the "free market."

Tennison's persona as an ordinary person wears thin by the time senior U.S. senators praise her, when she meets in a Kremlin office next to the president's, or when Russia's best-known TV personality shows up for her court appearance in St. Petersburg (a pipe in her apartment burst and caused damage downstairs). Nonetheless, she won attention and respect as a citizen without official status, with the help of hundreds of volunteers.

Sharon Tennison is modest about her abilities as a litterateur, and the latter part of her book is organized more like a fascinating diary than a set of stories with a clear arc, but taken as a whole, *The Power of Impossible Ideas* is engaging, suspenseful, inspiring. She and her colleagues were happy warriors for peace, and her book recounts the kind of adventure story that actually happened.

At the close of the book Tennison summarizes the huge differences between the learning, relating, and negotiating styles of the two peoples, based on their very different histories. If the first lesson of citizen diplomacy was "we're remarkably similar," the later understanding among those who stuck with it was "we're quite different but can learn from one another, get along, and even enjoy it."

# CHAPTER 29

# A Nuclear Secret

O n a citizen diplomacy trip to Moscow in October 1986, I learned a disturbing secret about the Cuban missile crisis that shocked even Robert McNamara when he first heard the same Soviet secret six years later. The consequences of this secret continue to be relevant today.[18]

During the crisis in 1962, McNamara had been U.S. Secretary of Defense. My Soviet source, Fyodor Burlatsky, had been a close aide to Nikita Khrushchev—who had sent missiles and warheads to Cuba and decided, at the climax of the crisis, to remove them. That crisis, which lasted thirteen days for the U.S. side, has been called the most dangerous moment in human history.

What Burlatsky told me, over coffee, was that before the climax of the crisis, the Soviets had already brought to Cuba not only big missiles that could reach much of the U.S., but also, unknown to JFK and his aides, tactical nuclear weapons for delivery systems that could be used to repel a U.S. naval invasion of the island.

As I knew from Robert Kennedy's account (published in 1969, after his murder), U.S. leaders gave serious consideration to launching an invasion of Cuba—and had made preparations to do so. According to Michael Dobbs in *One Minute to Midnight* (2008), arguments in favor of invading Cuba were presented by the President's National Security Advisor McGeorge Bundy, by members of the Joint

Chiefs of Staff, by Senators Richard Russell and J. William Fulbright, and by others.

After my meeting with Burlatsky, it never occurred to me that U.S. intelligence had not subsequently discovered the presence of Soviet tactical nuclear warheads in Cuba in 1962 (as perhaps they did after McNamara had left the Pentagon). It seemed likely that my Soviet source was trying not to scare me, but to find a way to prevent a future miscalculation, to reduce the probability of something like the Cuban missile crisis ever happening again. I regarded the information as an example of the new and uncertain policy of *glasnost*, or openness.

My modest contribution was to suggest that the former Khrushchev aide, along with other principals and staff on both sides, could meet and share what each of their perceptions had been during the crisis. I also suggested some possible sponsoring organizations, mainly academic. A series of meetings ultimately did occur, including the one held in Havana in 1992 at which McNamara first learned about the tactical nuclear weapons.

In that Havana meeting when Fidel Castro revealed the truth about the tactical nukes, McNamara was extremely upset and later said he "couldn't believe what I was hearing," thinking perhaps the translation was bad. He asked Castro three questions: Did the Cuban leader know in 1962 about the Soviet nuclear warheads then on the island? Would he have suggested that the nukes be used against the U.S.? And if they were used, what did he think would happen to Cuba?

According to McNamara, in the frank atmosphere of these retrospective meetings Castro replied that he did indeed know during the crisis that the Soviets had brought nukes to Cuba, including the ninety tactical warheads. And Castro had, in fact, suggested to Khrushchev that nuclear missiles in Cuba be fired at the U.S. At that point, Castro went on to say that if his advice had been taken, he fully expected his country to be totally destroyed. Further, Castro offered the opinion that if McNamara and JFK had been in a similar situation they would have acted as he did.

In Errol Morris' documentary movie *The Fog of War: Eleven Lessons from the Life of Robert S. McNamara* (2003), the former Secretary of Defense is shown pausing, at a loss for words, overcome by emotion as he reports that he replied to Castro; "Mr. President, I hope to God we wouldn't have done it. Pull down the temple on our heads? My God!"

My amiable coffee with Fyodor Burlatsky in Moscow happened more than twenty-three years after the missile crisis, so any secrets from that episode were no longer operational but archival in nature. Nonetheless, the lesson about the rich possibilities of miscalculation remains relevant now.

Why was McNamara so upset? Until that meeting in 1992, he had been unaware the Soviets already had tactical nuclear warheads stationed in Cuba (although U.S. intelligence had discovered delivery systems for tactical warheads), and he was upset because one option seriously considered by the President's special executive committee was an invasion of that island nation. Preparations were actually being made, and when the crisis was settled, the planned invasion of Cuba had been only a couple of days away.

Dean Acheson, who had been a distinguished Secretary of State under President Harry Truman and who, as an elder, was invited into U.S. deliberations during the Cuban missile crisis, called the outcome "pure dumb luck." But if JFK had followed Acheson's advice—and that of several members of his inner circle, top military leaders, Senators, and others—to attack as many of the known missiles as possible and then to invade the island; and if the Soviets had fired even some of the tactical nuclear weapons they had (including one aimed at the Guantanamo base), where would a nuclear exchange have stopped?

McNamara, who had favored the idea of a blockade of Cuba adopted by JFK, and who like Acheson did not know about the Soviet tactical nukes, also eventually realized how much luck had been involved in the outcome of the crisis. In *The Fog of War*, while slashing his hand at the camera McNamara says, "It was luck [pause] that prevented nuclear war." Holding his index finger a quarter inch from his thumb, he adds, "We came that close."

The point for today is that when nuclear weapons are involved, we are one step away from irreparable consequences. A friend of mine defines humans as "quasi-domesticated primates with power tools." And, as Jonathan Schell warned us in *The Fate of the Earth* as long ago as 1982, the tools now include a collection of nuclear missiles capable of casting into the shadows even World War Two and the events of those years.

A mythology grew up about JFK's crisp performance as a crisis manager, but the dominant lesson learned by the best and brightest was that when in a crisis, you should show some restraint: Don't "pull down the temple" as McNamara said, or "tug on the ends of a rope in which the knot of war has been tied," as Khrushchev described. Instead, consider your options carefully and offer the other side an acceptable deal.

At the end, the way out of the Cuban missile crisis was a U.S. initiative via an agreement under which the Soviet missiles would be swiftly removed from Cuba in return for a promise that American forces would not invade that island, along with a secret verbal promise that the U.S. would withdraw missiles from Turkey in four to five months. Since the latter missiles were old fashioned and vulnerable anyway, the U.S. considered that it had prevailed. As McNamara reported in *The Fog of War*, when he brought the Joint Chiefs of Staff to the White House, JFK informed them that our side had won—but they were also instructed to be tactful and not claim victory.

Perhaps if JFK had not allowed the prior Bay of Pigs invasion to be launched and then aborted, and if he had not permitted Khrushchev to treat him roughly at the 1961 Vienna Summit, Khrushchev might have hesitated to ever send nuclear weapons to Cuba. In that case, there would have been no crisis to manage.

A nuclear war, represented by what Khrushchev called a knot, would have meant destruction for both superpowers (and for places where they had military forces), and probably a nuclear winter as well. According to McNamara, that knot was barely untied.

Apart from the necessity of having cool heads during a crisis, or to pick the option that works, what is the lesson of McNamara holding his fingers slightly apart and saying, "we came that close" to nuclear war? Will good crisis management and luck really be enough in the long run?

In financial analysis, "black swans" have become a popular metaphor for dangers that are very high in negative consequences, even if they seem quite low in probability. Examples of this include the behavior of big banks and the economic crisis of 2008; in terms of nuclear power, Chernobyl and Fukushima; with storms, the effects of Katrina; deep sea drilling, the BP geyser in the gulf; or in terms of rocketry, the Challenger disaster (which had happened in the year when I first visited Moscow).

These crises share a theme: The very low estimated probability of their happening. Obviously, they *did* happen. But has this lesson been learned? In the documentary about him, McNamara remarks that he knew of *three* situations that nearly ended in a nuclear exchange.

Since the years after 1991, the U.S. has preened itself as the sole remaining superpower, but the world is still full of nuclear weapons, including warheads in the hands of enemies of each other (India, Pakistan), a potential rival of ours (China), what is called a rogue state (North Korea), plus the core of the former U.S.S.R. (Russia), European allies of ours (France, Great Britain), and Middle East states (Israel and, perhaps in the future, Iran).

Apart from their existence, at least some of these warheads and many nuclear materials are ill guarded and, in any case, subject to the kind of secrets and miscalculation that occurred in the Cuban missile crisis.

## CHAPTER 30

# Out of Almost Everywhere

Many people want to get the remaining U.S. troops out of Afghanistan; some want us to get out of almost everywhere.

The rise of the American military empire and the reasons for winding it down are examined in a trio of books associated with a website called *TomDispatch*.[19] From the brilliant proprietor of the site, Tom Engelhardt, comes *The American Way of War: How Bush's Wars Became Obama's*; and from two of his frequent contributors we have *Washington Rules* by Andrew J. Bacevich and *Dismantling the Empire* by Chalmers Johnson, a coda to his pioneering and celebrated "blowback trilogy."

These books overlap in spirit, though each focuses on a different question. Bacevich, for example, in discussing what he calls "America's path to permanent war," points out at one time the U.S. was reluctant to get involved in foreign adventures unless attacked, but after decades of building a network of bases and (despite a loss in Vietnam) embracing an ideology of intervention, now accepts the concept of preventive war and "enhanced interrogation techniques" that would allegedly enhance our safety here at home.

Engelhardt assembled some of the best of his pieces from *TomDispatch*, like "Air War, Barbarity and Collateral Damage," and "Is America Hooked on War?"—as hooked as an addict, he concludes. (Articles contained in this feast of a book can also be read on the web in the TomDispatch.com archives, which go back to 2002.)

Chalmers Johnson, described by Engelhardt as "the most astute observer of the American way of war I know," describes less about how to dismantle the empire, despite the title of his book, than about why we should urgently do so. He builds not only on his startling trilogy, but also on the work of investigative reporters and historians such as Steve Coll, Tim Shorrock, and Tim Weiner.

With the caveat that each member of the trio associated with scovers somewhat different aspects, let's examine some propositions that inform all three of them:

The U.S., which thinks of itself (and which presents itself) as an anti-imperial power, maintains a global network of more than 700 foreign bases, which can be regarded as a kind of empire.

This network, along with a military budget equal to much of the entire rest of the world combined, encourages us to intervene in other countries as we did in Vietnam, Iraq, and Afghanistan.

In most cases these interventions have been costly failures for us, and disasters for people there.

We could do better by spending the money not on "military Keynesianism," but on domestic infrastructure, social needs at home, and new industries to address urgent problems now largely neglected.

U.S. presidents want to appear "tough"; members of the officer corps, to have opportunities to do what they are trained for; and members of Congress to get reelected, in part by bringing military spending to their districts.

Our news media, with some exceptions, does a wretched job of covering the empire, military spending, wars we fight, and the effect on our republic of a system based on secrecy.

"Until we decide (or are forced) to dismantle our empire, sell off most of our bases in other people's countries, and bring our military expenditures into line with those of the rest of the world, we are destined to go bankrupt in the name of national defense." (Chalmers Johnson)

Despite these stakes, the ideology of intervention and the military budget (or as Andrew Bacevich says, "Washington rules") are no more profoundly questioned in our capitol than the ways of our financial system or our de facto energy policy.

Even if a president wanted to end this system, he or she would be boxed in by "political engineering," of which the Pentagon is a master, by the threat of popular generals to challenge the White House, and by the belief, widely shared, that the U.S. can do whatever it wants.

"Until candidates begin losing because angry Americans reject our perpetual wars ... this sort of thinking will simply continue, no matter who the Commander in Chief is." (Tom Engelhardt)

Apart from access to resources, the U.S. sometimes fights mainly to oust a regime it can't control; or even, once it enters or starts a war, to prevent damage to its prestige.

Most Americans fail ever to see our actions as others do, preferring to believe in our good intentions rather than to examine actual results.

The fanfare for the supposed end of the war in Iraq neglected the "enduring" bases, the large number of remaining troops, the almost invisible "contractors," and the huge, fortress-like "embassy."

The effort to replace a failed state in Afghanistan with a government friendly to the U.S. is doomed by lack of an adequate partner and an Afghan military and police that are willing and able to provide security for a central government; by the hatred engendered by what our side dismisses as "collateral damage"; by our efforts to stop the main cash crop of the country (opium); and by the proven ability of Afghans to hold off foreign occupiers such as the British and the Soviets.

Even if we could accomplish our mission in Afghanistan, terrorists have many other failed states in which to find safe harbor.

A limitation of these books is that they don't tell how to roll back the military empire—except for some implications and cursory suggestions—but the great strength is that they provide a coherent picture you'd never see if you depended on most of TV and the mainstream press.

What is the alternative to the system that's evolved? According to Johnson, in the tenth of the steps he quickly outlines, "We must give up our inappropriate reliance on military force as the chief means of attempting to achieve foreign policy objectives."

Inspired by George Kennan, Senator J. William Fulbright, and Martin Luther King, Jr., Bacevich argues that "The proper aim of American statecraft ... is not to redeem mankind or to prescribe some specific world order, nor to police the planet by force of arms," but rather, "to permit Americans to avail themselves of the right of self- determination as they seek to create at home a more perfect union" and a way of life based on "humane" values.

# CHAPTER 31

# World on the Edge

I t's okay to warn or complain, but one of the attractive habits in American civilization is to ask, "Well, what's your plan?" In his book, *World on the Edge: How to Prevent Environmental and Economic Collapse* (2010), Lester Brown offers one.

While watching the global life support system for a few decades, Brown warned us about specific gathering troubles, eventually articulating a plan that has gone through several iterations to the point where he now proclaims that it will take a "massive mobilization at wartime speed" to prevent economic and environmental collapse. The cover of *World on the Edge* shows a glacier calving a hunk into the sea, a sight that I once witnessed in Alaska—a tad awesome if you're in a kayak.

The chapters on particular troubles are familiar to anyone who has been reading books and reports from Worldwatch Institute, which Brown founded in 1974, or from Earth Policy Institute, which he started in 2001; I will focus instead on his solutions.

So what does Brown want us to do? After chapters on how to deal with failed states and environmental refugees; to seek energy efficiency and alternative sources to replace fossil fuels; to do our best to feed eight billion hungry people; to alleviate (or even eradicate) poverty; he ends with a chapter on "saving civilization." Here, in just twenty pages, Brown delivers his plan in brief:

"We need to build a new economy, one powered with carbon-free sources of energy—wind, solar, and geothermal—one that has a diversified transport system and reuses and recycles everything."

But how, you may ask, do we get there? Brown begins by proposing a market that would "tell the truth through full-cost pricing." This in light of the fact that despite squawks in favor of "free" markets, many of the costs of burning fossil fuels are not paid by those who sell the fuel, or by those who do the burning. Economists call these costs "externalities," which is a fancy way of saying they are "paid by somebody else, off the radar screen, and not brought up in polite company."

And in the case of fossil fuels, these externalities include, but are not limited to (as a lawyer would say), challenges to good health, environmental effects (mountain-top removal for example), the portion of the "defense" budget devoted to assuring a flow of fossil fuels, tax breaks and subsidies for energy corporations. Above all, externalities include the effect of carbon dioxide ($CO_2$) on producing, albeit with a time lag, global warming and thus climate change.

Brown calls for a carbon tax "to reflect the full cost of burning fossil fuels," which would somehow be offset by a reduction in income tax. But offset whole, or in part? The game was revealed by one of the first President Bush's economists, who wrote that such a tax shift would lead to "less traffic congestion, safer roads." How? Drivers would be reducing our miles on the road (and perhaps our speed). In other words, most of us would become less affluent, at least in terms of mobility. Poorer, at least, compared to what's now easy to get.

Poorer. This is the word few dare to utter. As the British

journalist George Monbiot explains, nobody ever rioted or demonstrated for austerity. But if the price of oil is going to rise as world production reaches the downslope (especially if demand, as in Asia, rises), then we are going to have less mobility, at least in the form of what James Howard Kunstler satirically calls "happy motoring."

Brown has watched as the real costs of our economic growth—of burning gasoline and coal, of deforestation, of over-pumping aquifers and overfishing—are undercounted, including the externalities is his formula for a rational economics. "If we can create an honest market," he claims, "then market forces will rapidly restructure the world energy economy."

The problems are two: Energy companies may praise and even see themselves as engaged in, and gain by using the rhetoric of, a supposedly free market, but they benefit from diverting attention (like magicians) from all the externalities that distort the markets they're actually in. Also, their customers don't want to pay more for gasoline, say, or electricity from fossil fuel powered generating stations. The net result is the markets remain distorted, we pay disguised costs, and our debts are transferred to the future.

Brown likens our economic system to Enron, which, he says, "devised some ingenious techniques for leaving costs off its books."

The author has adopted free-market rhetoric, while asking that all the excluded actual costs of the system be brought into the price. For example, if all the external costs of gasoline were to be added to the roughly $3 per gallon paid in the U.S. at the time his book was written, according to Brown it would have to cost $15 a gallon. Even if part of this increase were offset, and even if the offset included people who don't pay much or any income tax, most people couldn't drive as much as we presently do. However, as Brown says, "These are real costs. Somebody bears them. If not us, our children."

The real issue is, excluding some so far unknown technological miracles, the peak of production of traditional oil means we are going to become poorer in terms of the goods and services we can buy—a decline that might be masked by monetary inflation. This is the hard truth almost nobody wants to face. A decline is tolerable in case of war, or a business cycle, or some brief emergency, but even in a civilization not based on the "American dream," a long-term decline might be unwelcome, even devastating.

How we deal with a decline, if it occurs, will define us. Will we try to hold on, pretending that the living standard graph is just temporarily pausing before its inexorable rise? In terms of purchasing power, the income of many people has been on a plateau for as much as thirty years. And although the illusion of growth can be maintained by borrowing, by importing cheap goods, and by increasing the number in a household who are working, how would we react to a decline that wasn't just a brief recession?

This would bring to the top of the agenda the fairness and effects of wealth distribution in the U.S. in *World on the Edge*, Brown gently excoriates our economic system, which he says "neither recognizes nor respects sustainable yield limits of natural systems," a fault famously shared with Soviet communism and the systems the Chinese have developed.

Brown devotes more than a quarter of his plan for saving civilization to coal-fired power plants, perhaps because they have a long life and, once built, would be pumping $CO_2$ into the atmosphere for decades. Remember, a mobilization would have to be not only massive, but speedy. "Can we close coal-fired power plants fast enough to save the Greenland ice sheet?" asks Brown. If that melted, the sea level would rise about twenty-three feet and, as a result, "Hundreds of coastal cities will be abandoned. The rice-growing river deltas of Asia will be under water."

But Brown is not discouraged, with his long experience of looking the monster in the face. Yes, we have to mobilize, he says, but we did that after the sneak attack on Pearl Harbor. Alas, if something that dramatic were to happen in the natural world, "by then we might be over the edge." Brown places his hopes on a grassroots movement, like the one for civil rights, a kind of movement that he calls "ideal."

What would the movement demand? The civil rights protesters demanded to be treated as first-class citizens (and in the later stage, to have the same economic advantages as other Americans). In the last pages of his book, Brown presents a rough budget for universal basic health care, protection of biological diversity and of topsoil, reproductive health and family planning, restored fisheries, universal primary education, and other initiatives, which together would total only 28 percent of the U.S. military budget. He would redefine national security in these terms, rather than only (or even mainly) in terms of ability to coerce and destroy enemies. He says that in 2009, the U.S. military budget was 43 percent of everything spent on the planet in this category.

Brown ends by pointing out that individual decisions about what we choose to buy for our households will not be enough. I recall seeing Al Gore's film about "inconvenient" environmental trends, *An Inconvenient Truth*, and my disappointment that the suggested remedies were so timid—as if we could save the world by installing compact fluorescent bulbs!

# Global Warming

# CHAPTER 32

# The Global Crisis

Each era is unimaginable to the era just before, except to a tiny circle of visionaries such as environmental author and journalist Bill McKibben, founder of the group 350.org which works tirelessly to alert others to the impact of global warming. Some of these visionaries are misguided, but McKibben bases his diagnosis on scientific evidence that has momentous implications for our "way of life."

*Eaarth,* with its doubled second vowel, is McKibben's deliberately drawling name for the planet we now live on, which is, he argues, no longer the planet on which we were born. The change is nothing as obvious and immediate as an oil slick in the gulf or as limited to one spot on the map—it is gradual and invisible, not unlike many cancers. Being invisible, it is deniable, at least for a while. "How could I be afflicted in my prime by cancer? There must be some mistake."

We're in trouble, writes McKibben, but we're still focusing mainly on undeniable perturbations, such as oil spills and the global debt crisis—undeniable and relatively minor. If we can encourage the "green shoots" and return to vigorous growth, our leaders assume, everything will be okay. But McKibben argues in his book that growth, part of the civic religion of the U.S., must be replaced—not by the wishful concept of "sustainability," a concept he rejects as "squishy," but by contraction and a sense of what he calls "enoughness." So what's the good news? According to McKibben, the good news is that, while it's too late to prevent terrible damage from climate change and the peak of traditional oil production, we can use our ingenuity to manage the contraction "gracefully"—the ultimate message, and last word, of his book.

Although McKibben uses the term "global warming," a phrase that terrifies a climatologist but sounds tolerable to most people, he understands that the trouble will be experienced as *climate change*. Nature will reallocate water, as it has already begun to do—some agricultural areas will wither in drought, while other places suffer torrential rains and hurricanes. Rivers will dry up or flood. Infrastructure will be damaged; food production cut, at least food supplied by the currently dominant means. Oceans will rise, fed by water from melting glaciers.

The 1970s would have been a good time to begin a swift transition to a new economy. We had a president, Jimmy Carter who, at moments, expressed our predicament with regard to energy. Back even before the young McKibben was writing "Talk of the Town" pieces in *The New Yorker*, we were given a series of books, whatever their shortcomings, that might have forewarned us and pointed to some alternatives. These included works by Donella and Dennis Meadows and their colleagues, *The Limits to Growth* (1972); E.F. Schumacher, *Small is Beautiful: A Study of Economics as if People Mattered* (1973); Ernest Callenbach, *Ecotopia* (1975); Denis Hayes, *Rays of Hope: The Transition to a Post-Petroleum Age* (1977); Amory B. Lovins, *Soft Energy Paths* (1977); Ivan Illich, *Toward a History of Needs* (1978); William R. Catton, Jr., *Overshoot: The Ecological Basis of Revolutionary Changes* (1980); Duane Elgin, *Voluntary Simplicity: Toward a Way of Life That's Outwardly Simple, Inwardly Rich* (1981); and Wendell Berry, *The Gift of Good Land* (1982).

But the triumph of Reagan in 1980 made it clear that a majority was not yet prepared to halt the party fueled by the dramatic spike in energy available from fossil fuels, a spike which so far has lasted about two centuries. Coal, oil, and gas have allowed us to be warmer in the winter; to build an electrical grid fired by coal, and then also by natural gas; to build a fleet of cars and modern roads; to fly in airplanes; to make plastics and various industrial chemicals; and rounding out this list of examples, to bring fertility to soil using ammonia produced by the Haber-Bosch process. What's not to like?

Of course the answer is carbon dioxide ($CO_2$), an invisible by-product of burning all this fuel. Could the combustion from millions of sources, taken together, hold more of the sun's heat in our atmosphere and thus shift the climate? According to McKibben the answer is yes, and the focus of his book is the trouble caused by that heat.

Along with many allies, McKibben found a way to stimulate a worldwide demonstration about climate change. He began with something that might seem unpromising: The number 350, the maximum parts per million of $CO_2$ that atmospheric physicist James Hansen said would preserve the longtime conditions in which civilization has flourished. Before the time of the Industrial Revolution, the concentration of $CO_2$ in our atmosphere was only 275 ppm; just prior to the publication of this book, in 2016, it reached 400 ppm, an ominous sign of what might be ahead.

According to 350.org, the website of McKibben's campaign, "Unless we are able to rapidly return to below 350 ppm this century, we risk reaching tipping points and irreversible impacts such as the melting of the Greenland ice sheet and major methane releases from increased permafrost melt."

Or, we could add while speculating about "positive

feedback," the added heat absorption caused by the melting of reflective Arctic sea ice still covering dark water.

In this most valuable book, McKibben returns us to the theme of *The Limits to Growth* and thus questions the central dogma of our civic religion—as big a heresy as when in the early sixteenth century a Polish polymath questioned the belief, supported by the Church of Rome, that the Sun revolved around the Earth.

McKibben's prescriptions are not unfamiliar, in part because of his own voluminous writing. He favors rebuilding local economies instead of imagining that we can sustain globalization; growing food by means other than industrial agriculture (including local, organic farms and millions of suburban gardens); developing an economic system around the values of durability, robustness, and enoughness; gaining the stimulation of travel in larger part via the Internet; building social capital; and above all, reducing not the rate of increase in greenhouse gases, but the absolute proportion.

We know how to increase the gross domestic product, but (to allude to the title of one of McKibben's earlier books) is our system capable of producing *just enough,* and of distributing it fairly? It's easier to label the news of climate change as a hoax, and to dismiss the messenger as a hypocrite, or worse, a misguided nerd. It's easier, like a defense attorney, to raise doubt about the evidence, and in this case, to capitalize on the dutiful doubt that is the hallmark of good science.

Part of the value of *Eaarth* is the generous array of examples from all over the world gathered from extensive reading, organizing, and travel (in this case, let opponents of greenhouse gases have as big a carbon footprint as their work requires, say I). Part of the value flows from the courage of casting doubt on economic growth as the mantra of a successful civilization of the future. And part is McKibben's companionable, coherent, and good-humored account of our fix, delivered in the tone you might hear in response to a question from a well informed friend on a hike as he steps over the sticks, gracefully.

# CHAPTER 33

# A Suit for the Emperor

I n an iconoclastic talk at the University of Bristol, a leading
British climate scientist invoked the lad in Hans Christian
Andersen's story of the emperor's new clothes. In the story,
swindlers offer to make a new suit for the emperor of magic
fabric that they announce can't be seen by people who are
stupid or "unfit" for their positions. Although the swindlers
weave nothing, everyone in the court is afraid to expose
the fraud until the vain emperor, wearing his new invisible
outfit, goes on parade and a child shouts that he's naked.

In alluding to this story, Kevin Anderson began a talk
that, in its tone, could be described as the passion of a rational
man casting himself as the truth-telling child, the world's
political leaders as the emperor, and scientific policy advisers
as the weavers, or rather, as people who (for whatever reasons)
tell less than the whole truth about climate change.

Well informed by other scientists and engineers Anderson,
a professor of energy and climate change, is deputy director
of the UK's leading climate science consortium, the Tyndall
Centre. His claim in the talk was that, far from exaggerating
the danger, some scientists close to policy makers acquiesce
while politicians and their helpers describe the situation as
being less dangerous and less immediate than it is. To the
extent this is true, politicians (and their constituents) are
less than fully informed of what changes are necessary, and
how urgent is the need.

In particular, Anderson points to the goal of a two-degree centigrade rise in global mean surface temperature, a mantra accepted at international conferences including Copenhagen, and by his own government in the UK. According to Anderson, this goal is unmeetable unless we take extreme measures, and yet it has brought about no adequate action to date. Instead, he says we are on track for a four-degree rise, or worse. It's as if prudent governance is paralyzed.

To nearly all non-scientists, a four-degree rise sounds acceptable. After all, we deal with extreme variations in temperature between night and day, winter and summer. But to a climate scientist, four degrees is known to be a calamity. The reasons are many. Four degrees is an average over the whole globe, most of which is relatively cool water; and some land areas will be more affected than others. Second, climate change will mean that some areas have disastrous floods, while others, including agricultural lands, suffer drought along with temperature increases that threaten crops. Third, the oceans will rise, imperiling coastal cities such as New York as well as hundreds of others around the world. Fourth, tropical diseases will migrate north.

In the British transcript of Anderson's talk, apart from the stark conclusions, the most haunting word is just a noise made by the speaker, transcribed repeatedly as "hmm." It's hard to know what this sound means. Is the speaker wondering how to convey the urgency of what he's seen? Is one fact tumbling over another? Perhaps the speaker is musing over what will possibly break through the good-natured resistance of people whom he feels are thinking "This can't possibly be happening."

Anderson's prophetic voice is directed at the place where climate science and politics meet. According to him, we are sleepwalking in a fantasy land where we pretend that a two-degree rise is no big thing, while, he says, keeping the rise that small would actually require heroic measures starting now. In his talk, he pointed out that what counts is not the gases emitted in some far off year, when we say they will finally be low, but the cumulative emissions from now until that point.

He knows that purveyors of doom are not welcomed, so, near the end of his talk he asked, "What can be done?" In one graph he imagines a deliberate 10 percent reduction in emissions each year, but he observes that even when Russia's economy collapsed in the 1990s, the annual reduction was only 5 percent. In short, the situation is as extreme as a global war.

It seems impossible that something as beneficial as fossil fuels could hurt us, could through its emissions at worst take the advanced world back to the time before the Industrial Revolution, and then much further. Meanwhile, we tend to deny, temporize, or talk about adaptation. Even if our serious droughts and hurricanes are not caused by global warming, or even worsened, they demonstrate to some degree what nature might do; and they are the kinds of events scientists predict will be affected by warming.

Anderson has a conclusion that is simple: (a) emissions are not caused equally by the seven billion people on the planet (soon to be nine), but most of it by just 10 percent (or even less) of global population, and (b) emissions need not be a long-term problem, but the transition to a low-carbon economy must happen soon. So, what he advises is a short-term change, quite large, focused on the rich countries.

In Anderson's analysis, the solution lies in the world's richest people using less energy and thus becoming less prosperous—or to put it another way, less rich. This cuts against people's desire to have as much as we can manage, and cuts too against the myth of progress. Why shouldn't we always have more, as measured by gross domestic product?

The field of economics has flourished in a world in which, apart from wars and the pauses called recessions, consumption has grown. The financial system, we are being told, works only in this condition, because loans have to be repaid with interest. The American dream, which is now also a Chinese dream, assumes that each generation, on average, will be more prosperous than the last.

But historically, prosperity depends on energy. Energy now is mainly carbon based. Carbon endangers the climate. Politicians talk as if a return to growth will solve our problems, by creating jobs, increasing discretionary income, producing tax revenues. When we grow, we're happy.

There are two problems with this: As the easy-to-access fossil fuel energy is used up, the cost of extraction rises, or "peaks." But even to the extent that we can afford this energy it produces emissions, which at best impose enormous costs—and at worst imperil our future.

One response is to call these facts a hoax. Another is solemnly to agree on an impossible task: To keep global mean surface temperature rise to two degrees centigrade and then do nothing to reduce domestic emissions except export manufacturing processes that emit greenhouse gases, and have a recession.

The merit of Anderson's position is that he says what would be necessary, even if it seems "politically impossible." It is not up to him, as a scientist, to say how the necessary can be done. Likewise, we cannot reliably expect leadership from those who face election (and re-election) and fear backing an unpopular course.

We are now on track for implementing desperate attempts to adapt to new conditions, like expensive projects such as seawalls for New York City, followed by desperate attempts at global atmospheric engineering.

This challenge is difficult in that it's not as obvious as a response to a surprise attack on Pearl Harbor. The cause is invisible gases. The accumulation is gradual. The gases are caused by activities whose benefits are obvious, even taken for granted, and we have built our way of life around these benefits. The fossil fuels we use are supplied by giant corporations that have a cash flow that can easily pay for the disinformation ads, campaign contributions, and lobbying they do in order to defend their economic interests. The "green" energy substitutes require a huge new infrastructure, and might not provide as much energy as the fossil fuels.

Effective action will require collective or governmental steps, not just voluntary "consumer" decisions. Nobody wants to be put at an economic disadvantage by taking steps while others gain market share by continuing to pollute. But above all, who wants to pay more for energy?

# CHAPTER 34

# When Elites Fail

Elites in both corporations and government are often quite good at running systems they create, but bad at looking beyond these systems at larger social effects. This tendency was on display at the Worcester Polytechnic commencement in Massachusetts back in 2011.

For its main speaker, the college had invited Rex Tillerson, CEO of Exxon. A group of students and faculty, disturbed that fossil fuel purveyors are causing great harm to the planet, exercised the right of protest. One student said, "We will not give the Exxon CEO the honor of imparting his well-wishes for our futures when he is largely responsible for undermining [our futures]."

This group invited their own speaker, Richard Heinberg[20] of the Post Carbon Institute and author of *Powerdown, The End of Growth*, and eight other books.

Tillerson gave an unexceptional address as he spoke of Worcester embracing "the cutting edge of technology," having colleges train more scientist and engineers, encouraging graduates to have personal integrity, and the need for students to take time off from their Blackberries every day. While he did allude to "creative financial schemes" that "destroy billions of value in pensions and other investments," he had nothing to say about the peak of traditional oil production or the environmental costs of burning fossil fuel.

Those who ducked out to hear the "alternative" speaker got an earful. In less than 3,000 words Heinberg told about challenges that will require much more than personal integrity. He began by reminding his audience that U.S. traditional oil production has been declining since 1970, and according to the International Energy Agency in Paris, global crude oil production peaked in 2006, leaving oil, as Heinberg explained, that is lower in quality or located in places harder to access.

Saying that he had not flown across the country to "demonize" Exxon, Heinberg nonetheless accused the company of "adopting the tobacco industry's disinformation tactics and funding some of the same organizations that led campaigns against tobacco regulation in the 1980s." Organizations that are now busy denying the scientific evidence of climate change.

In his address, Tillerson told the graduates to respect "the integrity of the scientific process." But Exxon, said Heinberg, has funded organizations that cast doubt on that process and "raised doubts about even the most indisputable scientific evidence" while attempting "to portray its opposition to action [in response to climate change] as a positive quest for 'sound science' rather than business self-interest."

Heinberg went on to tell the students the success of this disinformation campaign was "a disaster for democracy, for the Earth, and for your generation." Saying that commencement speaker Tillerson knows as well as anyone that "the world will have to transition off fossil fuels during this century," Heinberg argued that delay is "extremely dangerous." Delay means not only more entrapment of solar energy by greenhouse gases, but also a loss of the time needed to build a renewable energy economy. In that case, he sees the prospect of "a trap of skyrocketing fuel prices and a collapsing economy."

Heinberg, pointing to the gap between the interests of firms such as Exxon and the interests of society, said "When the price of oil goes up, we feel the pain while Exxon reaps the profits." He also discussed how, in addition to funding climate change denial, fossil fuel companies like Exxon have "contributed to politicians' election campaigns in order to gain perks for their industry and to put off higher efficiency standards [for vehicles] and environmental protections."

According to Heinberg, the amount that Exxon invested in 2010 in a so-called Global Climate and Energy Project is no more than it paid in personal compensation to its CEO.

Explaining that renewable sources of energy each have "limits and drawbacks," Heinberg said for this reason "we will probably have less energy in the future." He predicted the new graduates "will see world changes more significant in scope than human beings have ever witnessed before."

While the Exxon CEO was telling graduates to act with integrity, Heinberg named two enormous challenges their generation will have to face:

- Growing food sustainably for the more than seven billion people we can expect to be on the planet in the near future.

- Reorganizing the existing financial system so it can "perform its essential functions, reinvesting savings into socially beneficial programs, in the context of an economy that is stable or maybe even shrinking due to declining energy supplies, rather than continually growing."

To the extent Heinberg is right, people identified with fossil fuel energy are part of an elite that illustrates this double truth:

- They are resourceful at finding, extracting, transporting, refining, and distributing their products; and at maximizing the profits of their firms while extracting subsidies from governments and engaging in international manipulations to reduce taxes.

- With regard to the social cost, this same clever and hardworking elite is a failure, in part because it doesn't define social costs as its business. Pressed, it may claim that an "invisible hand" reliably converts private greed into social good.

Thus, we have built systems so complex that, with few exceptions, only the relevant elite understand them, and yet that elite is devoted not to the public good, but to "shareholder value" or some ideology.

Another illustration is the national security elite (admirably well educated, shrewd, tough minded) who, at the end of the Cold War, after the Berlin Wall was breached in 1989, claimed nobody could possibly have predicted an end to the struggle that had persisted for more than four decades, yet there were *many* people on both sides who didn't waste time predicting but devoted their energy to trying to find an alternative.

I know this to be true because of having had the honor of giving grants to some of the groups in the U.S. that were working hard to establish ties with the Soviets, and of developing a shared vision of another kind of relationship. These groups included the Esalen Soviet-American Exchange program, Beyond War, and Sharon Tennison's Center for

Citizen Initiatives that ran "Soviets, Meet Middle America" and many subsequent programs.

The national security elites on both sides managed to avoid nuclear war, though several times it was barely averted. They operated the system called the Cold War quite well, but the point is they were not equipped to find a way out of it.

Whether it's the fossil fuel energy managers, or the masters of national security, an elite may successfully run the system that it has created, while never trying to find an alternative. That is the task, as Heinberg made clear, that now falls in part upon the generation born around 1990, which has the prospect of being only sixty-years-old in the middle of the twenty-first century.

## CHAPTER 35

# Our Renewable Future

A re we who are aware of our current global climate crisis resigned to repeating a sad litany of the Arctic melting, wildfires raging, weather getting weird? Of tipping points, new expressions of denial, and all the rest of it? Or are there any models of enormous beneficial changes that may appear at the last minute? I'm thinking of something bigger than the Montreal protocol, which succeeded in shrinking the ozone hole and thus gave us false hope that authorities would also deal with other climate troubles.

Short of U.S. entry into World War II, which was occasioned by a surprise attack, the closest example that I know of was the near-agreement at the Reykjavik summit in early October 1986. I happened to be in Iceland at that time, on my way as a "citizen diplomat" to Moscow, when that meeting of world leaders ended suddenly, with disappointment evident on the faces of Mikhail Gorbachev and Ronald Reagan.

Their negative emotions were understandable as this was a last minute failure of an agreement that would have done something truly historic by eliminating all nuclear weapons within a decade, and thus ending the standing threat of "mutual assured destruction."

I later found out what had happened when the National Security Archive released both the Soviet and U.S. "memoranda of conversations" recorded by official note-takers in the conference room. (To a remarkable degree, the two sets of notes agree.)

Apart from note-takers and translators, the two superpower leaders were meeting with no staff other than the Soviet foreign secretary and his counterpart, George P. Shultz, the U.S. secretary of state. When Gorbachev and Reagan reached a verbal agreement to eliminate all nuclear weapons, Shultz, who was nicknamed "the Buddha" for his implacable demeanor, nonetheless blurted out, "Let's do it."

Because the nuclear system remains largely out of sight, many people do not realize how dangerous it's been. Well-informed U.S. observers such as Secretary of State Shultz, two secretaries of defense (Robert S. McNamara, William J. Perry), and National Security Advisor McGeorge Bundy, when separately asked why no nuclear war had occurred, gave the same answer using the same word: "luck."

What is interesting about the Reykjavik Summit is not the failure, but the near-agreement on a step of world-altering scale. The agreement was foiled only by Reagan's insistence that research on his program to achieve a defense against nuclear missiles be permitted not only in the laboratory but also outside. Scientific analysis at the time concluded that such a defensive system would be very hard to develop and easy to fool, with, for example, fake warheads.

Why did Reagan otherwise agree to eliminate all nuclear weapons? Did he feel there ought to be a defense? Was he certain that the Soviets would never agree to his condition?

It's often forgotten that the summit came after three amazing events. In 1982 Knopf published Jonathan Schell's book, *The Fate of the Earth*, a call for nuclear abolition. Also in 1982, building on several years of widespread organizing in the U.S., the nuclear freeze movement initiated by Randall Forsberg held a huge rally in Central Park—the largest rally in U.S. history.

And in November 1983, NATO conducted a war game called "Able Archer." The Soviet leader Yuri Andropov suspected the exercise was cover for a surprise attack on the U.S.S.R., and was ready to launch a preemptive attack on the West (all this would have been observed by Gorbachev, who was elevated to General Secretary in March 1985). In Moscow in late 1986 I learned about another nuclear near-accident (see Chapter 29) from a man who'd been at Nikita Khrushchev's elbow during the Cuban Missile Crisis.

I am writing now not primarily about nuclear policy, but rather about the equally difficult predicament of global warming. Of course it's easy to find differences between the two: Nuclear war has always been a clear if hidden danger while global warming seems like a future threat. Also, at the time of the Reykjavik meeting, the nuclear threat could have been settled by two world leaders meeting around a small table in Reykjavik's historic Hofdi House; in contrast, global warming is caused by greenhouse gases emitted all over the globe.

However, there are also big similarities, and in both of these cases powerful lobbies have an economic interest in the status quo. In the case of the nuclear "triad" (bombers, missiles, subs), that lobby was (and is) what Eisenhower called the "military-industrial complex." In the case of global warming, it is the fossil fuel industries, here and abroad. Just as our civilization depends on coal, oil, and natural gas, so we relied (and still rely) on the nuclear threat for our security. This retaliation system yields benefits—unless it fails.

After the Orlando, Florida mass shooting in 2016, my local paper quoted people in the street who called it "unimaginable."

Of course the slaughter wasn't unimaginable, statistically it was almost predictable, but we humans don't have a very good record of envisioning what we don't want to see, or what our ideologies can't deal with. And in extreme form this reaction becomes denial. Toward this kind of behavior it's tempting to feel superior, but in regard to our current climate crisis, while many of us honor the evidence and support the science telling us it is indeed reality, what do we actually *do* about it?

One of the organizations that has been wrestling with this beast for years is the Post Carbon Institute, founded by Richard Heinberg and friends. The institute's book by Heinberg and his colleague David Fridley, *Our Renewable Future: Laying the Path for One Hundred Percent Clean Energy*, has enormous value that is derived from three qualities: (a) it vividly imagines a positive outcome, skipping over the well-known dangers that can be avoided by its achievement;(b) it realistically reduces the challenges to engineering problems, explained in some detail; and (c) it forthrightly calls for certain sacrifices to be made in our current lifestyle with less per capita energy.

"A point we have raised repeatedly," wrote Heinberg and Fridley, "is that possibly the most challenging aspect of this transition is its implication for economic growth: whereas the cheap, abundant energy of fossil fuels enabled the development of a consumption-oriented growth economy, renewable energy will likely be unable to sustain such an economy." Renewable sources won't replace all the services provided by fossil fuels, and the Post Carbon book does not re-imagine the use of nuclear power (referring to that industry as "moribund"), but prefers instead to view a more realistic emergence of clean technologies accompanied by reduced energy use.

Have we hesitated to deal with the lower energy output of renewables by focusing on the enormous harm that will eventually be caused by greenhouse gas emissions? If so, what has been the result? People are allowed to feel the crisis caused by global warming is far off, and another generation's problem. Meanwhile, they worry about heating their homes, getting to work, having a steady supply of electricity, receiving goods from the "globalized" economy, getting food, and all the other tasks now performed with the help of fossil fuels. In any case, they feel powerless, especially in a system in which surveys show large majorities favor policies that the government does nothing, or not enough, about—gun control, universal healthcare, the cost of higher education, and gross inequality.

Can we draw a loose analogy between Jonathan Schell's book and thoughtful studies such as *Our Renewable Future?* Between Randy Forsberg's "nuclear freeze" in the 1980s and the current work of Bill McKibben and many others on global warming? Between the near-agreement at Reykjavik and a future success that would lead to a transition to a renewable energy regime? As citizen diplomats often said, "If the people lead, leaders will follow." But it will take a mass arousal such as we've rarely seen, based on a vision of a successful transition, to accomplish the task at hand.

I'm reminded of a job offer at lunch in 1984 with a wealthy man. He wanted to endow and help run a foundation with a single goal of helping to end the Cold War, and to prepare a book in support of that goal. When I gently observed that the goal would be very difficult to reach, he replied, "I know it seems impossible, Craig, but it is necessary."

One of our means then was citizen diplomacy, reducing the isolation between the two superpowers, focusing on shared values, imagining an era of peace. Now perhaps one need is for a citizen's movement based on the idea of a successful transition to a renewable energy system. That's what Heinberg and Fridley are offering.

# CHAPTER 36

# Who's Got the Social Inventions?

G lobal warming challenges us to go beyond the use of ordinary political tactics to the level of social invention. Ordinary tactics can be heroic, seemingly all we have, and even effective up to a point, but in this case we may need to supplement them with tactics not drawn from past struggles.

A new social invention channels energies through a social, legal, or economic arrangement that didn't previously exist. We may think first of technological innovations such as TV, the commercial jet, the personal computer, or the smartphone. But we've also been amazingly good at social inventions like the Louisiana Purchase in 1803, and later the Homestead Act which was signed by Lincoln in 1862 and helped to populate the frontier by giving away about 10 percent of the land in the U.S. More recent examples of social inventions include tax deductions for philanthropy and use of the Internet to create social media and crowdsourcing.

But a much longer list can easily be made, starting with ideas that appeared in the *Declaration of Independence*. Thomas Jefferson, one of the great social inventors, gave us not only the Declaration but also a charter of religious freedom, his home state's university, and the aforementioned Louisiana Purchase—the acquisition of the whole middle of this continent from the claimant, a harried and distant

France. Did the U.S. Constitution say that the president could buy enormous tracts of real estate? It didn't, but it didn't say he couldn't. Jefferson's legacy is a series of social inventions, the kind of acts that people call "politically impossible," and their offspring, enjoying annual fireworks, take for granted.

Internationally, a few examples of social invention are the Marshall Plan for the reconstruction of Europe after WWII, the UN Declaration of Human Rights, agreements not to use certain kinds of weapons, land devoted to national parks, the Grameen Bank for microloans. We can argue about the effectiveness and net benefits of any of these social inventions, but they suggest the kinds of arrangements we need to consider in order to deal effectively with climate change.

And while conventional politics can help, so far the results have been drastically insufficient. What we currently need is a network of social inventions on a global scale.

It has long been a cliché to call for another "Manhattan Project" to develop new sources of energy, or to lessen the burden of greenhouse gases put into the atmosphere, or both, but this kind of development would be technological, rather than social. We may need both kinds of inventions.

Barriers to conventional solutions are huge. Fossil fuel firms have fought, and will continue to fight, to preserve their dominance won by providing much of the energy that made possible the wealth of economies that are already "advanced" and "rapidly developing." The propaganda and political influence of these corporations is amplified, as noted elsewhere, by hundreds of millions of citizens who must purchase fossil fuel for running cars, trucks, ships, farm equipment, and airplanes; for heating houses, offices, and factories; and for producing industrial chemicals and other products. People are terrified of any steps that might hurt our present economy.

Al Gore tried to be our Winston Churchill as he gave speeches, testified at hearings, and presented scientific evidence in the film *An Inconvenient Truth* to warn the public about the climate effects of business as usual. In the 1930s, as a member of parliament, Churchill had gathered intelligence about Adolph Hitler from worried civil servants, travelers, and others, and made a series of well-informed and urgent speeches challenging the prime minister of his own party by telling the awkward truth about German rearmament. But the UK government was committed to a policy of not challenging Hitler, both because mobilization would upset the economy and, most of all, because almost nobody wanted another debilitating war.

During a summer in Oxford I saw on the wall of a college cloister many rows of names of students who were casualties of the war of 1914, and one of my walking companions who grew up in Yorkshire recalls the amputees on the street corners of his boyhood. England denied what was going on in Europe in part because of a memory, only two decades in the past, of trench warfare that killed so many husbands, sons, and brothers.

With regard to climate change, we sometimes seem to be waiting for a wartime Winston, the indomitable leader who, having warned in vain, declared that his people would never give up, would tolerate whatever bombs the enemy might send, would repel any invasion force. At the Imperial War Museum in London, housed in the former insane asylum called Bedlam, I once pondered the grim situation that Churchill faced in 1940 when he told the country he could offer only "blood, toil, tears, sweat." Because the government hadn't listened to him, he didn't have adequate arms.

Reluctantly, in many cases, his listeners made the switch from trying to be nice to Herr Hitler to rearming and seeking allies. But after the country failed to act on Churchill's warnings, it could easily have lost the war despite the prime minister's fortitude, if Hitler hadn't invaded his "ally," the Soviet Union, and if Japan hadn't attacked Pearl Harbor.

One problem of waiting for a wartime Winston, with regard to climate change, is that we can't count on the equivalent of the Russian people wearing down the Nazis by absorbing incalculable losses, or the U.S. being roused out of isolationism by direct attack. It is the nightmare of climate change analysts that by the time the danger is obvious, there will be no remedies available. We will make a seamless transition from "there's no problem," or "it's a challenge for the grandkids," to "it's too late."

To illustrate the difficulties of dealing with climate change, imagine the immediate resistance, in normal politics, to a "carbon tax" sufficient to make sustainable energy economically competitive. Our political system is slow to impose even a slight increase in already low taxes paid by the rich, and has a noisy element opposed to *all* taxes, as well as an aversion to "government" itself. Can we expect any adequate response to climate change by ordinary means?

Some situations that look impossible actually are impossible, but some aren't. For example, nobody expected the end of the Cold War, and when it came, at least for a while, some national security experts in America thought it was a trick. The causes of the end were complex, but one of many elements was "citizen diplomacy," which gave the Soviets hope that an alternative existed into which they could move. The history of citizen diplomacy is routinely neglected, except in such books as Sharon Tennison's *The Power of Impossible Ideas.*

We "know" that foreign policy is made or influenced not by unofficial contacts or by visions of a positive future, but solely by tough calculations of trade and arms (what the Soviets called "the correlation of forces"). In the sphere of vested interests, the problem of global warming seems intractable.

Can we somehow find social inventions that lead to a viable future? Are there ways for people to invest in a future that will be different from our present, to become identified with it, to work for it, to build a new way of life while detaching from the old? Are there, in short, social inventions that would allow us to dis-identify from a dysfunctional pattern and to identify instead with ways that will work?

In the past we've made beneficial social inventions on a massive scale. They are as American as apple pie. So who's got the social inventions now that we really need them?

# CHAPTER 37

# Liberty Bonds: Bringing Ordinary People into the Energy Transition

What can ordinary people do to help start a serious and rapid transition to renewable energy, and thus to a reduction of global warming?

Looking back to the early 1980s, I recall that although ending the Cold War was widely assumed to be impossible, several changes broke the logjam, including the needs, vision, and daring of Mikhail Gorbachev. And, on the U.S. side, despite Ronald Reagan's early rhetoric as president, we had the "nuclear freeze" movement with a campaign of local initiatives culminating in a monster rally in New York City's Central Park and the publication of Jonathan Schell's book about nuclear abolition, *The Fate of the Earth*, both in 1982; a TV movie about the ghastly effects of a nuclear strike on heartland U.S.A., *The Day After*, broadcast to a huge audience in 1983; ground-breaking citizen diplomacy beginning in the early 1980s; an astonishing summit meeting between Gorbachev and Reagan in Reykjavik in 1986; and "Soviets Meet Middle America," which was part of an extensive exchange program that began in 1988.

I too was able to play a role when a wealthy San Francisco Bay Area entrepreneur and philanthropist invited me to work with him through a new foundation dedicated to the single goal of helping to end the Cold War standoff. My admiration for his initiative led to a pair of books, *Citizen Summitry and Securing Our Planet*, financial support for some thirty groups, trips to Moscow plus an appearance on Soviet TV, and around a hundred appearances in the U.S. by the co-authors of the books.

Along with street demonstrations, TV, and the rest of the useful hoopla, one thing that was new about the era was a huge program of citizen exchange between this country and the Soviet Union. Observing from the Bay Area we were impressed by the Esalen Institute program, as well as by a new venture pioneered by Sharon Tennison whose deeply revealing book about this under-reported phenomenon is called *The Power of Impossible Ideas*.

Citizen diplomacy provided what lawyers call a "form of action"—a way of doing something. U.S. citizens could travel to the other side, and vice versa. With the help of a Gorbachev appointee who provided exit visas, Tennison brought unofficial Soviets to hundreds of cities in the U.S. where they were hosted by "middle Americans" who brought them to backyard barbecues, schools, houses of worship, small businesses, radio stations. In the same way ordinary Americans, instead of stopping in Western Europe, could go a little further, land in Moscow, and meet ordinary Russians. Politically, this awakening helped to give the leaders something to move into. As citizen diplomats used to like to say: "When the people lead, the leaders will follow."

What changed? People who would otherwise have said "I know, but what can one person do?" were now provided with a form of action in which they could relatively easily participate.

In facing climate change, rather than denying it or acting

as if it's a problem for somebody else, later, can we create forms of action for ordinary people—soon? For example, could a bond program be created in support of a rapid energy transition the way war bonds (also called Liberty Bonds) were used to support the military effort in the 1940s? These "Energy Bonds" could be bought by ordinary people and used to buy and install renewable energy devices (solar panels, wind turbines, and other modalities) as they become available.

The bonds would be repaid out of the revenue streams from these devices, and out of secondary purchase of the devices themselves, with the goal of making them easily accessible starting immediately after the program begins. These new energy sources could be owned in a variety of ways: by corporations (some may be non-profit), by municipalities, and by private homeowners. People who choose to buy a bond will be part of the rapid growth of renewable power, and these same folks will be able to communicate with their neighbors about their evolving experiences with the new technologies.

This is only an illustration of a form of action that would appeal to ordinary people who, despite the propaganda spread by fossil fuel industries trying to repeat the success of the tobacco lobby, know that they and their children will be better off after a rapid transition to clean energy. The point is we can't wait for the political elite to act, considering the extent to which they are bought off by campaign contributions and grotesquely large speaking fees—as well as by the misleading climate change denial of so-called "think tanks."

In the absence of forms of action for ordinary people to engage in, we will witness the spectacle of increasingly less cautious scientific warnings, natural disasters (wildfires, floods), absurd self-congratulation by diplomats after weak agreements like the Paris meetings (COP21), all followed by panic when it's too late to act. The need for an energy transition is so much bigger than issues such as abortion, or gross economic inequality, or other matters that currently arouse such passion—of what use would these be in an unlivable world?

It is hard to explain the lack of action on climate change, which I have elsewhere called the "issue from hell." Is the difficulty because a rapid switch to renewable energy would leave us with less energy than we're accustomed to using, and thus inevitably raise the issue of gross economic inequality? Is it because those who respect the scientific consensus are satisfied with merely laughing at Donald Trump? Is it because a serious solution involves not only major changes to transportation, but also to the raising of methane-emitting animals for food, and the preserving of rain forests? Is it because of the temporal gap between the emission of greenhouse gases and their ultimate effects, which leads some observers to predict continued complacency followed by panic? In any case, global warming remains relatively low on surveys of public concerns after such items as the provision of good jobs.

Whatever role will be played by street demonstrations, becoming involved and making a difference in this "invisible war" will require ordinary people taking actions that can't be easily blocked by the fossil fuel industries. A vigorous program of energy bonds is just one possibility; local initiatives, such as those suggested by this book, are also essential to solving our planetary crisis.

# Tough Times Scenarios

# CHAPTER 38

# Perils of Geoengineering

I f the climate and energy debates were a house, what would be the "elephant in the living room"? (A phrase referring to a lumbering presence that's almost too dangerous to discuss.) So what would play the role of the elephant? Is it the hope, often unspoken, that technology will save us? That if our globe is warming some miraculous technique, perhaps not yet even known, will be developed and deployed just in time? That thanks to the promise of human ingenuity, we don't have to reduce emissions of greenhouse gases produced by enormously useful and omnipresent fossil fuels? That we can continue, at least to the extent that the economy revives, with business as usual?

This hope must serve as at least part of the reason we haven't panicked. It lies deep in the American psyche that when we have exhausted all other alternatives, we will be saved by a "machine from the gods" (to reverse a phrase from ancient drama)—or rather by a technique from scientists and engineers.

This kind of last-minute salvation happened during our harrowing fight against the Axis powers during WWII, when we needed to know where German subs were and thanks to a genius named Alan Turing our side was able to break the enemy's naval code; and when the allies needed warning that hostile planes were approaching, radar was invented.

So, why reduce greenhouse gases if a technique will

almost surely (or probably, or perhaps possibly) be developed that makes it unnecessary? For decades scientists and others have floated various ideas for cooling the atmosphere, something now referred to as geoengineering, or "hacking the planet," as science reporter Eli Kintisch says in his brilliant book *Hack the Planet: Science's Best Hope—or Worst Nightmare—for Averting Climate Catastrophe* (2010).

Geoengineering proposals take several forms, such as trying to reduce the solar radiation that reaches the earth by "brightening" clouds with a spray of seawater from below; or simulating a volcanic eruption by seeding the stratosphere with sulfur particles (or some other chemical).

We might try to increase the absorption of carbon dioxide ($CO_2$) to get more of this troublesome gas out of the atmosphere. Make and bury biochar (a soil enhancer made from organic waste matter that can hold carbon) as in the Amazon of old. Dump iron powder in the seas and create algal blooms. Develop artificial trees or improve the existing ones by bioengineering. Or, as biochemist Craig Venter proposes, bioengineer not trees, but microorganisms to gobble $CO_2$.

Or, we can try to prevent $CO_2$ from ever reaching the atmosphere by use of sequestration (trapping it and creating long-term storage), a wonderful challenge considering the cost and difficulty of capturing, pumping, and storing it securely. If practical, this technique would make a major difference: Dirty as it is, coal generates more than half of our electricity, and an even higher amount in China.

A scientist may be drawn to a technique that seems sweet or elegant; an entrepreneur to one that offers profit, perhaps from creating carbon offsets which reduce emissions made in one location to compensate for those made elsewhere; and a policy maker may favor a technique that facilitates business as usual, causing no alarm to economic interests that contribute to his or her campaign. And if the technique appeals to all three types of people, as some geoengineering project do, what's to stop it?

Well, experimentation on these methods hasn't gone very far, perhaps because of the obvious danger of unintended consequences. What stands out in Kintisch's first hand survey of the techniques is a pervasive uncertainty. Science may know the planet is warming, but doesn't know what to do about it other than reducing emissions globally. Or hope that efforts to hack the planet aren't disastrous.

On just one half of a page of Kintisch's book the following phrases appear:

- "the United Nations couldn't say"
- "scientists don't know"
- "certainty is rare"
- "it's unclear"
- "we don't quite know"
- "this chain of uncertainty... restricts the ability of scientists to predict accurately"
- "it's not an exact science"

In other words, it's as if we're trying to find our way in an unfamiliar thicket of birch saplings in heavy fog. The white of uncertain menace hasn't looked so threatening since Melville's pale whale.

Nonetheless, we hesitate to insist on the reduction of emissions in the hope that a technique can prevent or undo the ghastly effects of climate change. Without considering all the ramifications, just think of the effects of a devastating reallocation of water bringing drought to some regions, including fields that now yield food, and floods to other places not prepared for so much water (as has already happened in

Kentucky, Iowa, Texas, Louisiana, and other states).

Kintisch writes his book as a well-informed, open-minded reporter, dutifully covering both the hopes of the proponents of hacking the planet, whom he calls the blue team, and the stoplight warnings of critics, the red team. And, as his narrative makes clear, some of the "blue" players are nagged by questions while some of the "red" ones, knowing the situation, hope that something will work.

In Kintisch's view, a particularly troubling danger is that the sparkling promise of cheap geoengineering might function as a distraction from the serious, long-term work of reducing the emission of greenhouse gases. Another danger is that geoengineering experiments, and deployments, would be done in buccaneering style without adequate oversight, exploiting for commercial motives the commons of the atmosphere and the seas.

In the last pages, Kintisch reveals his personal conclusion: "Being forced to geoengineer would be a dismal fate" and "succumbing to the illusion of control" would mean replacing the burden of overhauling the world's energy system "with the much more risky burden of revolutionizing our relationship with the sky itself." A risky, dismal illusion of control. And, when we discover the less than obvious side effects, it might be too late.

# CHAPTER 39

# Chilling Out Globally

What has the atomic number of 16, and is liable, in the form of a compound, to be spritzed into the stratosphere by the mega-ton? You'd be right if you said sulfur. That's one of the interventions suggested by geoengineers to reduce global warming, along with such initiatives as making biochar from plant matter to remove carbon from the atmosphere, "sequestering" carbon dioxide ($CO_2$) under the earth, brightening clouds by spraying water upward, and dumping iron powder in the sea. A sulfur compound injected into the middle atmosphere would mimic a massive volcanic eruption, which is known to reduce the mean surface temperature.

Geoengineering is what humans could do after they've been unable to reduce emissions of greenhouse gases adequately, or are afraid to try, or feel that a reduction is not "cost effective." Some advocates say we should keep geoengineering in reserve in case of an emergency; while others urge us to do it pre-emptively, as an alternative to reducing the carbon emitted by tailpipes, smokestacks, and other industrial and vehicular sources.

After science writer Eli Kintisch produced *Hack the Planet in 2010* (see Chapter 38), which was a critique of geoengineering, Clive Hamilton, in *Earthmasters* (2013), added to the story with a special focus on ethics. In Australia, where he lives, Hamilton is branded as a public intellectual, which means he shares his extensive knowledge not only with his colleagues but with the educated public as well. A skeptic about humans, Hamilton called one of his prior books *Requiem for a Species*,[21] which devoted only part of one chapter to the idea of using atmospheric interventions.

Global warming has been on the agenda at least since 1988 when climate scientist James Hansen testified to a Congressional committee, and the next year when Bill McKibben gave us *The End of Nature*. Most climate scientists prefer reducing the emission of greenhouse gases to any form of geoengineering, but it isn't happening just yet—except as a result of economic recession. Fossil fuel firms warn that reducing emissions might wreck the economy, depressing the standard of living. So the carbon builds up, and geoengineering waits in the wings as a potential savior.

There are many reasons, however, as to why this idea is not yet ready to be safely implemented. Let's run through several difficulties.

First, by definition we don't know what unintended consequences would emerge if, for example, humans were to spray tons of a sulfur compound into the stratosphere. In medical terms, the cure might be disastrously worse than the disease. As you may recall, serious engineers and financiers judged the chances to be vanishingly low for an explosion of the space shuttle Challenger, the near-collapse of the U.S. financial system, or the multiple problems at Fukushima Daiichi in Japan.

Second, stopping some of the sun's radiation from reaching the earth would do nothing to reduce the acidification of the oceans, which like warming, is a product of carbon emissions.

Third, once this sulfur "shield" was created, it would have to be renewed: While $CO_2$ persists for centuries, the sulfur lasts only a few years. If after a while the spraying stopped for any reason, the global temperature would quickly rise, perhaps too quickly for the survival of some plants and animals.

Fourth, we have no international protocol specifying who can decide to spray sulfur, or any other substance. If such a momentous decision could be negotiated, why not negotiate a reduction of emissions?

Fifth, to whom would nations complain if they felt disadvantaged by the results of sulfur spraying? Who would judge their cases, what standards would apply, and who would pay damages? For example, what if there were a failure of monsoons and other rainfall needed for crops?

Sixth, and perhaps most seductive, if geoengineering were done pre-emptively, a bridge to the development and introduction of sustainable energy that is as cheap as natural gas or coal, would it not simply replace what it was meant to introduce? Even if methods of cheap low-carbon energy were invented, they would still have to be built as the new infrastructure.

Seventh, is geoengineering not just the latest Promethean project, when what we need are systems that Clive Hamilton calls "Soterian"? (His verbal coinage from the name of Sotera, the Greek god of "safety, preservation, and deliverance from harm.") President Nixon said the solution to any failures of technology is more technology, but Hamilton argues that is the wrong path.

True, the fossil fuel companies did not say "we'll push these substances on unsuspecting users who will crave them for immediate benefit, not looking to the future." Arguably they felt everyone profited as they helped build a civilization by supplying the coal, oil, and natural gas used in the steam engine, electric power plants, vehicles, furnaces, stoves, and various industrial processes.

The problem was, the vast immediate benefits brought a massive eventual flaw. It's hard to demonize the fuel suppliers without recognizing that *all* of us are their customers. They will defend their interests, fiercely, while we must recognize that our interests are now diverging sharply from that of these merchants of carbon.

This recognition comes at an awkward time: What's at risk is not only our customary source of energy, but also our civic religion. Whatever spiritual beliefs some of us hold, almost everyone worships at the altar of "progress." We expect that we will be able to buy more tomorrow than today; that our descendents will be better off, in perpetuity.

It is as if we've made a decision, by default, to risk that the findings of climate science are just a bad dream, or that a cheap form of sustainable energy will be developed, or that we'll find a way to defeat the economic interests of the fossil fuel industries, or that geoengineering will save us and not have unintended consequences worse than global warming. As a friend is fond of asking, "What can possibly go wrong?"[22]

# CHAPTER 40

# Transform While There's Still Time

In her book titles Carolyn Baker features such scary words as "demise," "chaos," and "collapsing," but her goal is mainly soul building.[23] The stressful outer reality is merely a provocation. In Baker's daily digest of challenging news ("Speaking Truth to Power," online at carolynbaker.net) she welcomes a whole range of "collapse aware" writers, including those who predict "near-term extinction." However her main vision is that, in the course of growing up, humans will sooner or later construct a better society—and in any case will live intensely in the present. She is like the stern teacher with a heart of gold.

In a similar spirit my men's group devoted itself, rather grandly, to "social invention" and called itself the "relentless optimists." I have mentioned a man who said during our search for a name, "There's nothing left but optimism." As he wryly meant (and as Baker means), what we need is nothing so deceptive and fragile as "hope," but a relentless descent into the turbulence of life and what Carl Jung called the "shadow."

"What fascinates me," Baker writes, "is not so much humanity's engulfment in darkness, but what kind of culture we will construct from the rubble of this one." While many people are still dazzled by the myth of progress, Baker sees our culture as "inherently abusive."

After working as a psychotherapist and a teacher of psychology and of history, she concluded that industrial civilization is ending, especially as she read about climate change, financial instability, and accidents in nuclear power. While understanding the kind of suffering this collapse would bring, she has a mission and a dream. The mission is to prepare people before their world falls apart, so they won't be surprised and lapse into panic and traumatic depression. Her dream is that a better society will arise as we wisely prepare for, and resiliently move through, a period of suffering.

One of Baker's many books, *Collapsing Consciously: Transformative Truths for Turbulent Times*, addresses how to prepare emotionally and spiritually for this inevitable collapse in the form of seventeen essays followed by fifty-one brief meditations. (As submitted, her manuscript had 365 meditations, but the publisher suggested keeping enough in the main book for weekly use and placed the rest in an eBook that uses the same cover photo and title plus the word "meditations.") Each of the short pieces begins with a quote from another author, after which Baker expands on the theme.

In an era of specialization, it's refreshing to encounter the fruits of wide reading. For example, Baker draws on activists (Rob Hopkins, Bill McKibben); classic authors (Fyodor Dostoyevsky, Emile Zola); current fiction writers (Annie Dillard, Flannery O'Connor, Michael Ventura, Alice Walker); historians (Karen Armstrong, the author herself, Elaine Pagels); movie directors (Ridley Scott, Steven Soderbergh); musicians (Cat Stevens, John Lennon); mystics (Hildegard of Bingen, David Steindl-Rast); natural ecstatics (Hafiz, Kabir); recent and contemporary poets (Denise Levertov, Antonio Machado, W.S. Merwin, Pablo Neruda, Rainer

Maria Rilke, William Stafford, David Whyte); psychologists (Carl Jung, Abraham Maslow); psychotherapists (M. Scott Peck, Bill Plotkin, Frances Weller); social observers (Barbara Ehrenreich, Duane Elgin, Derek Jensen, Rebecca Solnit); spiritual leaders and memoirists (Father Thomas Berry, Pema Chodrun, Peter Kingsley, Jiddu Krishnamurti, Eckhart Tolle); other workshop leaders (Angeles Arrien, Michael Meade, Margaret Wheatley); and those who write about the end of our current civilization (John Michael Greer, who contributed the foreword to *Collapsing Consciously*, Richard Heinberg of the Post Carbon Institute, James Howard Kunstler, Dmitri Orlov).

To cite a distinction made famous by Isaiah Berlin (about the fox who knows many things and the hedgehog who knows one big thing), Baker is foxy in her range of interests, hedgehoggy in her singular passion about our need to grow up as a species, to transform while there's still time. She sees a culture of two-year-olds, and feels we can do better.

This brings us to a peculiar category of human experience: The kind of challenge that almost nobody would dream of choosing but that, when thrust upon us and met, can yield gold—for example, a life-threatening illness. It's not something you can fully experience at a workshop (though Baker does lead groups in the exercise of imagining their own deaths), but a life-threatening challenge can ruin a person, or it can serve as an occasion for rapid and precious growth.

How does Baker see the challenge of collapse? In her view it won't be easy, but for those people who are prepared, it will deepen their souls and engage them more fully in life. Baker knows that people tend to define a comfort zone in which they feel competent, and then to get bored as they feel secure; or worse, to not even notice how bored they have become, how little they are developing. (See the second book in my Gratitude Trilogy, which is *Enlarging Our Comfort Zones*.) She encourages not warding stuff off but experiencing it fully, and venturing out to encounter more of the mystery.

If you respond to the meditations in the main book, consider downloading the eBook and enjoying the other 313 as you move through the year. One of them begins with an excerpt from Clarissa Pinkola Estes: "What do I know should die, but am hesitant to allow...? What must die in me in order for me to love? What not-beauty do I fear? Of what use is the power of the not-beautiful to me today?"

The prospect of collapse is not beautiful, but Baker shows us how to use it.

# Different Kinds of Spirit

# CHAPTER 41

# A Feminist Treasure

An unpublished treasure of feminist scholarship has come to light after years in a drawer in Rome. Written by an American expatriate, the book length typescript is called *The Serpent and The Storm God*. The author is Julienne Travers.

A copy found its way to my wife, who used to work in the Italian cinema and who long ago met the author in Rome. Together with an early circle of Italian feminists in 1970 they arranged an exhibition in the famous Piazza Navona, featuring magazine ads that showed women subordinate to men. Written comments made clear what was going on in the popular culture, and under Bernini's famous *Fontana del Quattro Fiumi* "fountain of the four rivers," they staged what might have been one of the first outdoor feminist protests, at a time when even divorce was still illegal in Italy.

The Piazza Navona exhibition (or what Italians call a *mostra*) involved a bit of benign misdirection. To get the necessary permit Travers put on a sexy dress plus a wedding ring (she was no longer in a marriage) and told an official that she and her friends wanted to celebrate women on Mothers' Day. The city official, swayed by the performance, signed the necessary permit making it legal for the feminists to use the famous piazza to show an alternative view of women, a view that Travers elaborates in her valuable book.

Travers was both an activist and, after work at the London

School of Economics, a private scholar. Her typescript has twenty pages of references, but the writing is not academic in the sense of dry; it is well documented but vigorous and, in places, tart.

Her theme is somewhat similar to Riane Eisler's landmark 1987 book, *The Chalice and The Blade*. Indeed, Travers' image of the serpent refers not to the Christian devil in the Garden of Eden, but to a pagan icon of feminine power. Likewise, Travers' storm god may call to mind the warrior energy that Eisler depicts as the "blade." Like Eisler, Travers portrays an admirable egalitarian civilization that was conquered and replaced by a hierarchical society brought by invaders from the steppes. Why does this matter? They both argue that what once existed can be constructed again.[24]

But in large part Travers' work is much more than just a historical curiosity preempted by others: She not only covers the transition from an egalitarian civilization to storm gods in more detail than other accounts intended for a general audience, but also, for example, deals in a special way with the goddess theme.

Some writers have played up the theme of women as goddesses: If men can promote gods, women, too, will have had divinities in their own image. Travers, instead, envisions not the deification of women in a prehistoric civilization, but a social structure in which no one is made into a divinity; there are only the symbols of the importance of a life force whose nature is female.

Travers portrays the concept of a "goddess" as an invention of invaders from the steppes, who understood only a hierarchical social order and thus assumed that the spiritual symbols of women in prehistory were symbols of great aggressive power—as they believed their totem, the eagle or storm spirit, to be. The invaders eventually projected on women's symbols the form of a supernatural female chief.

The egalitarian society's respect for horizontal social relations can be found in much of the Occupy Movement, which makes that movement so puzzling to those who have grown up in (and in some cases who depend on) vertical or hierarchical power-over.

# CHAPTER 42

# The Making of a Teacher

C an a lad sometimes regarded as bad by his father, by a Catholic priest, by the Army, and by the Drug Enforcement Administration transform in the middle of life's path into a Zen *roshi*? Can he then reinvent his tradition in ways that impress the brainy Ken Wilber, aka Mr. Integral?

*A Heart Blown Open* (2012) by Keith Martin-Smith shows how this did indeed happen as it follows the life of Denis Kelly from a small Wisconsin city to the San Francisco Bay area in its glory years, and then to a Buddhist monastery in upstate New York, with a brief stop in federal prison.

Why prison? On the West Coast, Kelly was head of a "family" that made available windowpane LSD, an adventure that allowed him to live the high life and to blow minds with well-refined molecules before he learned to help people blow open on the meditation *zafu*.

The biography reads less like a result of interviewing colleagues and examining documents than like the tales of a natural raconteur—with a good listener shaping the narrative and filling in some details. After a bout with cancer Kelly is very much alive, and is founder of the Buddhist order Hollow Bones. He spent an intense fortnight with Martin-Smith, who then drafted material and reviewed it with the primary source.

However, the result contains stringent judgments about the hero, many of them from Kelly's own lips. He apparently has a reputation to keep, not only as a "bad boy" but also as a Buddhist observer of himself and others. A few of the stories seem a bit truncated, but the bio offers more lively material than many books twice as long.

Kelly came to regard LSD less as a mountaintop and, like some authors in Allan Badiner's *Zigzag Zen*, more as a gate. He ultimately encountered limits in the practice he adopted, noticing that people who had "awakened" were sometimes held back by their emotions. For example, a person's behavior could be warped by unresolved anger.

While mastering the traditional *koans* (riddles such as the sound of one hand clapping), Kelly integrated yoga into the practice, pioneered what he called "emotional koans," and championed an ecological vision. For many people, his work followed the "training adventure" conducted by the Mankind Project, which teaches emotional literacy and awareness of personal mission (as described in Chapter 11).[25]

Martin-Smith's nourishing biography lays out food for thought about how experiences one might never have chosen can, with luck and hard work, lead to valuable psychological or social inventions. For example, what is the relation between dissociation caused by childhood trauma and beneficial witness consciousness? Between the rebel's view of life and the ability to lead people beyond the ordinary mind? Between seeing that "realized" masters can act badly and developing a broader basis for personal development? And what is the deeper wisdom in Bob Dylan's seemingly paradoxical line, "to live outside the law you must be honest"?

# CHAPTER 43

# Remembering a Psychotherapy Pioneer

"Applied Buddhism" is a surprising label for a school of psychotherapy, but according to the founder of the Hakomi Method, this tag fits. Take a man trained in natural science, expose him to eastern religions and to West Coast therapy and, in the hands of Ron Kurtz, the result was Hakomi.[26]

Kurtz died in 2011, after initially surviving a heart attack, and had said in his wry and paradoxical style: "If I get the opportunity, I'm going to kick Freud's ass." Kurtz had discovered the key to helping others heal was not the interpretation of dreams and stories, but the "loving presence" of the therapist. Instead of eliciting psychoanalytic material, he or she looks for bodily "indicators," which might be gestures, facial expressions, postures, or nervous tics.

Guessing at the kind of experience that might produce the indicator, the therapist proposes a "little experiment" in which the client is told that after hearing a simple statement he or she should share their first reaction. For example, if the person was avoiding eye contact (an indication of fearfulness) Kurtz might say, "You're totally safe here," guessing that the client's unconscious thought otherwise.

Attending to the phrase and noticing the first response requires, in the client, a state of what Hakomi calls "loving presence." This is where the Buddhist inspiration comes in. The mindfulness of the client and the loving presence of the practitioner are very like practices of the Buddhist meditator, and one of the eventual goals is similar: A kind of attentiveness, calm, and compassion toward self and others.

Hearing the quiet assurance that "You're totally safe here," the client might feel "Fat chance!" or "It's never been safe." This is a core belief, normally unconscious, and recognition of it usually brings up what Freud called the "repressed," though Freud elicited repressed material and dealt with it in ways very different from Hakomi.

Kurtz says that at this point it's the job of the therapist not to ask questions or offer clever interpretations, but to be quietly supportive, to wait, and meanwhile to supply the missing emotional experience (in this case, of safety). The process might go through many cycles.

Many of Kurtz's own sessions with clients were videotaped, and in some cases the tapes have been enriched by his commentary. It is astonishing, the speed with which repressed material comes up. And this happens not through dreams, jokes, or childhood stories, but through feelings when the therapist says a simple phrase that contradicts one of the client's core beliefs.

I met Kurtz in a small men's group called "the relentless optimists." When we were discussing the group's name Kurtz had said: "Yeah, I suppose you think things are so bad there's nothing left but optimism." While aware of global troubles about which we all get appeals for funds, Kurtz loved to laugh. "If a train crash is going to happen," he would say, "I will meanwhile have a picnic on the tracks." Unnecessary suffering was serious; for almost everything else, Kurtz had wit. One of the therapists trained by him posted a eulogy describing Kurtz as "genius … clown." The

Buddhist writer Wes Nisker might have invoked "crazy wisdom."

Kurtz enriched his school of therapy until the end of his life, reading widely, asking of each book or article "How can it improve Hakomi?" During breakfast at a local eatery he would discuss Daniel Goleman's reporting on destructive emotions, V.S. Ramachandran's findings on phantom limbs, or Ken Wilber's theories on everything, capped by a comic Henny Youngman routine over the oatmeal.

At his memorial service—where the tears were balanced, as at an Irish wake, by laughter—one of his students called Kurtz a "bodhisattva." Whatever he was, he told me that one reason for his humor was to deflect projections; another, to acknowledge how people actually are and thus offer comic relief from dealing with human suffering.

On the day of his wedding, he wrote a poem about taking refuge "in the law, the teachings, the good books, the holy writings of Buddhas, saints, preachers, drunk on love, who saw clearly, saw and sang ... "

In the period in which I knew him, Kurtz worked hard to simplify his method, to "refine" it. He left an institute in Boulder, which was based on his early basic therapeutic discoveries; a center in the town where he lived, based on his latest findings; and an international network. If you live in many parts of the U.S. (or Argentina, Australia, Canada, England, Germany, Ireland, Mexico, Switzerland), you can find a Hakomi practitioner who will help with the "refined" method of "mindfulness-based, assisted self-discovery." The institute also has a list of therapists trained in the original method.

# CHAPTER 44

# A Vision of Life
# Beyond Consumerism

Are there alternatives to consumerism? Other than something dreary such as the loss of a job, a prolonged economic downturn, or the stealth tax of inflation?

What is it, you may ask, this consumerism? It's the assiduous promotion of cravings that our economic system, at least until recently, has somewhat satisfied: "Your neighbor has it. You will be happy when you get it. You can have it now on easy credit." This amping up of desire for stuff is so normal now that it's hard to imagine any other approach to life.

Recently, I came across an old box with photos of my maternal grandfather and some clippings from his youth. There were already ads when he was young, but they seem so naive, displaying an object for its own sake, not associating it with sexy women, power, speed, or fierce animal species after which vehicles are named.

My grandfather had much less materially than my parents, but as I know from taking long walks with him, listening to his stories, playing games, and helping him build a boat, he was joyful.

I thought of him when reading *Confession of a Buddhist Atheist,* a book by Stephen Batchelor, author of the wildly popular *Buddhism Without Beliefs*. Buddhist practice teaches that life is full of suffering, and suffering comes from cravings. The trouble with cravings is that they often can't be satisfied and, when they are, the objects may vanish or degrade. And, in any case, they usually don't "make us joyful," or, if so, not for long.

In this view, a system of implanting cravings by sellers who hope to profit by them, of exacerbating desire, would be crazy. The question is: Why would you do that? Of course, people need the basics such as shelter, clean air and water, food, clothing, education, healthcare, the ability to work. But as Joe Dominguez and Vicki Robin asked in their classic, *Your Money Or Your Life*, to what extent does it serve you to mortgage your life to get more and more?

The service offered by Batchelor is to get to what he regards as the core of Buddhist practice, free of "accretions" imposed by various Asian traditions. Of course, some westerners are attracted to Buddhism in part by the rich baroque trappings of the Tibetans, the subtle Theravada traditions of Southeast Asia, or the spare paradoxes in Zen cultures. But other westerners want a practice they feel is more suitable for a scientific and democratic society.

Having been a monk in two of several Buddhist traditions in Asia (Tibetan and Korean), Batchelor sought what he regards as Buddha's basic realization. In his writing, he even sets aside such crucial elements of traditional Buddhism as rebirth and karma, not denying that the founder taught these doctrines, but attributing them to the Hindu world in which he'd grown up and arguing that they aren't necessary to Buddha's genius as expressed in the "Four Noble Truths."

Within Buddhism, Bachelor's heresy is not to do without the concept of divinity (the founder was agnostic about metaphysics), but rather to set aside any realm other than our life on earth and to accept the possibility of death as oblivion. This is a delicate point because the prestige of Tibetan religious leaders, starting with the Dalai Lama, depends in part on the claim of being reincarnated, and because the finality of death is almost unimaginable to most of us.

What a waste to obtain the necessities of life, guard against danger, form attachments to other humans and accumulate knowledge, and then poof, it's all gone like photo albums when a house burns down. This would be almost as unthinkable as a process of evolution; what human would design so slow, wasteful, and unfair a process? Batchelor's point here would be that the gist of Buddhist dharma practice is being aware of what's here, now, rather than placing hope, without evidence, in a happier life after death.

Insofar as we can see the situation of Gautama, he had been living the life of a prince. His house was not in foreclosure; he was not forced into the life of a wandering ascetic. The "middle way" that he eventually found was not forced on him by the global peak of oil production, by global warming, or by economic breakdown. He felt his realizatio,n or awakenin,g was superior to the affluent life of his time.

In the phrase of the brilliant British journalist George Monbiot, "Nobody ever rioted for austerity," which is acknowledged as a political fact in his book called *Heat: How To Stop The Planet From Burning*, about a painstaking and ambitious plan for reducing carbon emissions enough to avoid the worst ravages of global warming. A masterpiece of understatement, his phrase conjures the unlikelihood of a parade with placards calling for less affluence—but it fails to mention the widespread phenomenon of denial.

I don't know whether the Buddha ever rioted for austerity, but he certainly counseled against arousing rampant desire, especially as a way of life. But what can we do instead?

Change comes eventually less from a critique of a prevailing system than from the building of a new system; of something that doubters can enthusiastically embrace and help in the next stage of building.

In *Confession of a Buddhist Atheist,* Batchelor tells his personal story,[27] reaffirms his understanding of dharma practice, and offers speculation about challenges that Buddha faced in creating a new way of thinking and acting. This last task is especially tricky, because the writings called the "Pāli Cano"n are roughly as far in time from the founder as we are from Shakespeare. (Imagine if we had the plays only through an oral tradition.) But Batchelor asks himself, given what we do know, how would a man with Buddha's basic awakening proceed in the world of his time? We'll never know for sure, but a coherent account at least provides an armature on which to build.

To return to the original question: Is there an alternative to consumerism? If the future will be less affluent than the past, for whatever reasons—we don't know—will we cling to a system that is failing? Or will we have adopted new basic premises? And if the latter, what will the values be that don't depend on having a growing amount of stuff?

# Afterword

What a journey! It's clear that ordinary politics, by itself, is inadequate to respond to the great challenges that are arising. I don't know whether there will ever be an adequate response, but if so, it will take the form of social inventions, of new ways of being together, of passing through life. Sorry to be vague, but that is the way it is before requisite social inventions are developed and adopted.

The global situation can be viewed as an unfolding tragedy, or as an opportunity. Our ancestors have risen to challenges before, as at the time of the *Declaration of Independence* or the aggressions of Hitler and of the war party in Japan. It is one thing to praise "the greatest generation"; another, to become like it, to grow into the role.

Even though the cumulative effect may be dazzling, to enrich a town or city with social inventions *can* be fun to do. In contrast, while it is certainly daunting to make the social inventions that will handle the big challenges of today, it must be done. The alternative is inadmissible.

Remaining in denial until it's too late would be understandable, but no apology would later suffice. As they say in the Mankind Project, real men (and real people) step forward instead of pretending there's no challenge, instead of clinging to ideologies that have become perverse.

Social inventions can be made at any level. It's never easy to say that there's a better way; it's especially difficult to notice when business-as-usual is leading unintentionally, but leading nonetheless, to a bad end. But this recognition is the first step. Most people, nearly all people, are slow to believe that something successful in the past, and prevalent in the present, has become dangerous.

The social inventions featured in this book each depended on a leader, a person who saw a need and created a way to meet that need. After a social invention is widely accepted, we tend to forget that it may initially have been ridiculed or opposed—it becomes simply the way almost everybody behaves.

Elected representatives are not necessarily leaders, even when they represent those who elected them and not just those who paid for the campaign. Not everybody is a leader, just as not everybody is an artist. But many more people are more capable of leading, or helping, than they may assume. (My wife, a painter, has worked with many students who start by saying "I'm not creative," and then go on to do something wonderful.)

The big transition happens when you try. You make a social invention locally, and then it dawns on you that you have a power that can be applied on a larger scale. You draw upon whatever helps. You begin to define yourself differently. You are less an "activist" in opposition than an inventor suggesting, offering, inviting, drawing people together. While it's necessary and a blessing to stand in the path of evil, this book calls you to the exciting and positive work of social invention.

While physical inventions are often associated with profit-making enterprises, some social inventions exist in the realm of volunteerism, community service, and civic innovation. If we slide into tough times because of economic hardship, food shortages, monster storms, or other challenges which are out of our control, many social inventions that will help could be local—whether developed on the spot or borrowed from best practices elsewhere.[28]

If we focus on climate change, experts in the field distinguish between "mitigation," which means taking steps to reduce global warming, and "adaptation," which means trying to deal with the consequences of warming (and of feedback loops that magnify the effects). Mitigation is global because, wherever emitted, greenhouse gases spread through the whole atmosphere of the planet. Gases do not respect national boundaries, whether, for example, the boundaries of China, the U.S., or the European Union.

But adaptation to effects of greenhouse gases can be local, even when a national government attempts to provide help to localities. Thus, many forms of social invention are relevant on the local level. And one locality can borrow from another.

This brings us to the question of service. We live in an economy based on individualism and profit making, under the happy fiction that an "invisible hand" somehow reliably transforms the private quest for advantage and gain into social good. To the extent that our system breaks down, the idea of commonwealth may become more prominent, but how will we arrange for beneficial results, perhaps in the face of panic? The need for social inventions would then become more obvious.

Throughout human history, one ideology has given way to another. A familiar ideology may have served well in the past, at least served some people well, although it may be harmful if we try to hold onto it when conditions change, as they have. But that does not mean that an ideology that has opposed the old dominant ideology can serve us well in the new conditions. For example, an ideology based on so-called "free markets" and shrinking the government may have little to offer for effective action against climate change, and may therefore lead some people to deny there is a problem. However, this doesn't mean that "socialism" is the answer. It's time for invention.

The summer after college I had lunch with Bill Buckley, the two of us, in his office at the *National Review*, a magazine that he'd founded. Though we had different political views, our time together was less like a "firing line" than like an amiable mutual inquiry. I remember asking him what, behind his ideology, was his basic human value. After chewing another bite of his sandwich (we were brown-bagging), he replied "personal responsibility." It was a point of agreement.

This was long before global warming was an issue, except in some scientific journals read only by specialists. But I have often thought of his reply in the context of what we are now told by an overwhelming consensus of scientists. Without presuming to speak for anyone else, I ask, what is our responsibility now? Surely not to cast doubt on what has been called "inconvenient truth," but to freely inquire in order to develop a way of thinking that supports success.

# Endnotes

**Introduction**

1. One relevant book is *Social Dreams and Technological Nightmares: A Global Ideas Bank Compendium*, edited by Nicholas Albery (Institute for Social Inventions, 1999); and you may also wish to look at *The Book of Visions: Encyclopedia of Social Innovations* (Virgin Books, 1992).

2. I would love to have heard the conversation in 1804 when Alexander von Humboldt, the great scientist and explorer, went to the U.S. after his travels in South America and was received by Thomas Jefferson, then president. True, their conversation must have had limits—while the Prussian was strongly against slavery, Jefferson ran Monticello on slave labor—but the two men shared a strong interest in exploration. The year 1804 was the year after the Louisiana Purchase, the year that Jefferson sent Lewis and Clark on their journey to the West.

3. When I reported for my graduate school job, as a research assistant, the first thing I heard as the receptionist answered a phone call, were the words "human problems." This was the Institute for the Study of Human Problems at Stanford, founded by Professor Nevitt Sanford. I do not recall whether Sanford ever used the phrase "social invention," but he *made* several of these inventions, including the Institute and a subsequent version in Berkeley. The latter, called the Wright Institute, is today an accredited, free-standing school of clinical social psychology. (Of course the whole process of accreditation is itself a social invention.)

### The Grace of Social Inventions

4. Not to be coy, the town is Ashland, home of the Oregon Shakespeare Festival, near the Rogue River, on the Pacific Crest Trail. But my point is that the U.S. has many towns (and parts of cities) that can be home to new social inventions.

### Story-telling Evenings

5. A relevant how-to book is *Long Story Short: The Only Story-telling Guide You'll Ever Need* (Sasquatch Books, 2015).

### Learning for Elders

6. The Bernard Osher Foundation may be found online at http://www.osherfoundation.org/index.php?olli

### Power of Compassion

7. The account of, and context for, Kennedy's 1963 commencement address at American University in Washington, D.C. is available at: https://en.wikipedia. org/wiki/American_University_speech

8. *Gift of Darkness* is book one of The Gratitude Trilogy, which continues with *Enlarging Our Comfort Zones*, and then with the present book. Each book is self-contained and may be read without knowledge of the other two.

### Transition Towns

9. Rob Hopkins has also authored several books, all published by UIT Cambridge Ltd.: *Local Food* (with Tamzin Pinkerton, 2009), *The Power of Just Doing Stuff: How Local Action Can Change the World* (2013), and *The Transition Handbook: From Oil Dependency to Local Resilience* (2014).

**The Mankind Project**

10. Bill Kauth's book about the Mankind Project is *A Circle of Men: the Original Manual for Men's Support Groups* (new edition, Silverlight Publications, 2015).

**Mentoring in the Rose Circle**

11. Cara Walsh has also been involved in a center for restorative justice. Less familiar in the U.S., restorative justice is widely used in New Zealand's juvenile justice system.

**Boys to Men**

12. Boys to Men is part of a national network, which has a website at: http://boystomen.org/

**Mindful Molecules Section Introduction**

13. The 1960s research on creativity was reported in Willis Harman et al., 1966, *Psychological Reports*, volume 19, pp.211–227. In 2006, a team at Johns Hopkins rep orted a pioneering study by R.R. Griffiths et al., in *Psychopharmacology*, vol. 18(3), pp. 268–283. The title of their report was, "Psilocybin can occasion mystical-type experiences having substantial and sustained personal meaning and spiritual significance."

"Mystical-type experiences" and enhanced "creativity" sound promising for discovery of "better ways to live" for those who wish to consider employing this modality.

**The Sixties and Afterward**

14. Founded by Bob Jesse, the Council on Spiritual Practices (CSP) is one of a small network of US organizations that discussed safe, therapeutic, and sacred journeys using mindful molecules. Other organizations are The Multidisciplinary Association for Psychedelic Studies

(MAPS), founded by Rick Doblin and discussed in Chapter 18, and the Heffter Research Institute. Together they have sponsored conferences.

## Welcoming Warriors Home

15. To see Bill McMillan describing this process in an episode of the TV interview show conducted by the author of this book, as well as the documentary film directed by his wife Kim Shelton, go to: vimeo.com/19870882.

## Martin Luther King's Legacy

16. One of the great speeches of U.S. history was delivered by Martin Luther King at Riverside Church in 1967; both audio and transcript can be found at: http://www.americanrhetoric.com/speeches/mlkatimetobreak silence.htm

## The Freedom of Simple Living

17. Unlike many I failed to read *Walden* in high school, but upon arrival at my freshman room at Harvard found on the door a list of prior occupants and noticed the name of Henry David Thoreau, who had resided there in the 1830s. My sister joked that I was his roommate. I rushed out and bought the book. What most impressed me were not his evocations of the natural world, which had become commonplace, at least in some circles, but his advice in favor of simplicity, a word he repeated. Raised in a consumer culture, I found this almost revolutionary.

## A Nuclear Secret

18. Of course it would be stupid to attack any nation with the capacity to absorb a nuclear strike and retaliate effectively, but if we eliminated every stupid act from history we would be living in a very different world. This chapter examines a single instance of near war between nuclear

superpowers. There are others, examined, for example in my article "What We Can Learn from the End of the Cold War," published on the Internet by *The Huffington Post*. But this book is about positive initiatives, and this chapter is about a social invention—international conferences for officials involved on both side of the Cuban Missile Crisis. The goal was to go beyond Secretary of Defense McNamara's first lesson from his experience, "empathize with the enemy." The conferences allowed officials on both sides to talk directly with each other, in the same rooms.

## Out of Almost Everywhere

19. Tom Engelhardt edits a valuable website called TomDispatch.com, which presents long, well-informed reports by writers whom you seldom find in the mainstream press. His social invention is using the Internet as a way to reach a large audience with views not generally seen in most magazines or on radio or television.

## When Elites Fail

20. Richard Heinberg is founder of the Post Carbon Institute, located in Santa Rosa, California. Since *The Party's Over: Oil, War, and the Fate of Industrial Societies* (New Society, 2003; 2nd. edition 2005), he has produced a series of books on the need for a new energy system, including *Powerdown* (2004); *The Oil Depletion Protocol* (2006); *Peak Everything* (2007); *Blackout* (2009); *The Post-Carbon Reader* (with Daniel Lerch, 2010); *The End of Growth* (2011); *Snake Oil: How Fracking's False Promise of Plenty Imperils Our Future* (2013); *Afterburn* (2014); and *Our Renewable Future: Laying the Path for One Hundred Percent Clean Energy* (with David Fridley, 2016).

## Chilling Out Globally

21. In 2010, Clive Hamilton's previous book, *Requiem for a Species,* started with these words: "Sometimes facing up to the truth is just too hard. When the facts are distressing it is easier to reframe or ignore them. Around the world only a few have truly faced up to the facts about global warming. Apart from the climate 'skeptics,' most people do not disbelieve what the climate scientists have been saying about the calamities expected to befall us. But accepting intellectually is not the same as accepting emotionally the possibility that the world as we know it is heading for a horrible end. It's the same with our own deaths; we all 'accept' that we will die, but it is only when death is imminent that we confront the true meaning of our mortality."

22. After writing the prior draft of this chapter as an article for the Internet, then meant to be the final draft, I experienced the entire text disappearing in an instant during the upload, with no remaining version available. This unprecedented event astonished and angered me, until I paused to realize that the subject of the article involves a vastly worse loss, for many, than what had just occurred in my computer. The accidental disappearance of the familiar had, in a tiny way, a repairable way, reinforced the gravity of our situation.

## Transform While There's Still Time

23. In addition to *Collapsing Consciously* (2013), Carolyn Baker has given us a series of heart-wrenching books on the global crisis: *Sacred Demise* (2009), *Navigating the Coming Chaos* (2011), *Extinction Dialogs* (with Guy McPherson, 2014), *Love in the Age of Ecological Apocalypse* (2015), and *Dark Gold* (2015). For a good look at Baker, check out her

online interview with Janaia Donaldson on the brilliant video series at peakmoment.tv.

## A Feminist Treasure

24. For another wonderful book in the feminist tradition see *Motherpeace: A Way to the Goddess Through Myth, Art, and Tarot* by Vicki Noble, who, when I was starting as a book creation coach, became my first client. Her book remains in print a third of a century later.

## The Making of a Teacher

25. At the age of 60, on the hunt not for any "ism" but for a sort of mind training, I was introduced to Denis Kelly, a Zen roshi. He invited me to sit with his *sangha,* a circle of meditators that met almost daily around dawn, and that included individual talks with him in a form known as *dokusan.* While remaining ignorant of the stories in this biography by Keith Martin-Smith, I realized in the initial interview that Kelly had the air of a rogue, which was paradoxically attractive to me, because I wanted a teacher who exuded not piety but engagement with life.

## Remembering a Psychotherapy Pioneer

26. Ron Kurtz was author/co-author of three books: *The Body Reveals,* written with Hector Prestera, M.D. (1976); *Body-Centered Psychotherapy: The Hakomi Method* (1991); and *Grace Unfolding: Psychotherapy in the Spirit of the Tao-te-ching,* written with Greg Johanson (1991).

## A Vision of Life Beyond Consumerism

27. In regard to the book title, *Confessions of a Buddhist Atheist,* I suppose the word "nontheist" might have been awkward or confusing, but it would have been more accurate. Stephen Bachelor's other books include *Buddhism Without Beliefs* (1997), and *After Buddhism: Rethinking the Dharma for a Secular Age* (2015).

## Afterword

28. A San Francisco writer, Rebecca Solnit is author of *A Paradise Built in Hell*, a book about communities that arise in trying situations such as earthquakes, explosions, and hurricanes. Often, she finds, authorities expect anarchy in these situations, but people actually self-organize into helping groups. In tough times, people could panic, but they often transcend their culturally taught, self-interested behavior, which is assumed to be "human nature." Society's common assumption is that in an emergency people have no choice but to help one another, but the alternative interpretation, so haunting, is that the impulse is present in ordinary life, but seldom called upon. In effect, people create social inventions to get them through the breakdown, the emergency. In this sense, tough times are an opportunity. Solnit does not wish for disasters, having immersed herself in the study of several specific ones, but she notes that the elite are often surprised by how well many people behave, as well as by their impulse to help.

# Books Mentioned

*The following list, in alphabetical order by authors' last names, contains books cited in chapters and by guests on my TV show, plus a few other books that I'd recommend. In some cases, dates show not the original but the most recent edition.*

**Albery, Nicholas, and Stephanie Wienrich,** editors, *Social Dreams and Technological Nightmares* (Institute for Social Inventions, 1999)

**Alowan, Zoe, and Bill Kauth,** *We Need Each Other: Building Gift Community* (Silver Light Publications, 2011)

**Bachelor, Stephen,** *Buddhism Without Beliefs* (Riverhead Books, 1998)

**Baker, Carolyn,** *Collapsing Consciously* (North Atlantic Books, 2013)

**Brown, Lester,** *World on the Edge: How to Prevent Environmental and Economic Collapse* (Norton, 2011)

**Capossela, Toni-Lee,** *John U. Monro: Uncommon Educator* (Louisiana State University Press, 2012)

**Carlson, Don, and Craig K. Comstock,** *Citizen Summitry* and *Securing Our Planet* (both published by Jeremy Tarcher, Inc., 1986)

**Comstock, Craig K.,** The Gratitude Trilogy: *Gift of Darkness* (2015), *Enlarging Our Comfort Zones* (2016), *Better Ways to Live* (2017), all from Willow Press.

**Dobbs, Michael,** *One Minute to Midnight: Kennedy, Khrushchev, and Castro on the Brink of Nuclear War* (Knopf, 2008)

**Eisenstein, Charles,** *Sacred Economics: Money, Gift, and Society in the Age of Transition* (Evolver Editions, 2011)

**Eisler, Rianne,** *The Chalice and the Blade* (Harper, 1988)

**Engelhardt, Tom,** *The American Way of War: How Bush's War Became Obama's* (Haymarket Books, 2010)

**Fadiman, James,** *The Psychedelic Explorer's Guide: Safe, Therapeutic, and Sacred Journeys* (Park Street Press, 2011)

**Finkel, David,** *The Good Soldier* (Picador, 2010)

**Gore, Al,** *An Inconvenient Truth* (a film directed by Davis Guggenheim, 2006)

**Hamilton, Clive,** *Earthmasters: The Dawn of a New Age of Climate Engineering* (Yale University Press, 2014); *Requiem for a Species* (Routledge, 2010)

**Heinberg, Richard,** *Power Down: Options and Actions for a Post Carbon World* (New Society, 2004)

**Hochschild, Adam,** *To End All Wars* (Houghton-Mifflin, 2011)

**Jeavons, John,** *How to Grow More Vegetables* (Ten Speed Press, 2006)

**Junger, Sebastian,** *Tribe: On Homecoming and Belonging* (Twelve, 2016)

**Kintisch, Eli,** *Hack the Planet* (Wiley, 2010)

**Krznaric, Roman,** *Empathy: Why It Matters and How to Get It* (Tarcher-Perigree, 2014)

**Kurtz, Ron,** *Body-Centered Psychotherapy* (LifeRhythm, revised edition, 2007)

**Martin-Smith, Keith,** *A Heart Blown Open* (Divine Arts, 2011)

**McKibben, Bill,** *Eaarth: Making a Life on a Tough New Planet* (Times Books, 2010), along with the first book for a general audience about the climate crisis, *The End of Nature* (Random House, 1989)

**McNamara, Robert,** *The Fog of War* (an Errol Morris film, 2003)

**Metzner, Ralph,** *The Ecstatic Adventure,* with Alan Watts (Macmillan, 1968)

**Monbiot, George,** *Heat* (South End Press, 2007)

**Myrdal, Gunnar,** *An American Dilemma: The Negro Problem and Modern Democracy* (Harper and Brothers, 1942, and later editions)

**di Properzio, James, and Jennifer Margulis,** *Baby-Bonding Book for Dads* (Willow Creek Press, 2008)

**Quinn, Daniel,** *Beyond Civilization: Humanity's Next Great Adventure* (Broadway Books, 2000)

**Riesman, David,** *The Lonely Crowd: A Study of the Changing American Character* (Yale University Press, revised edition, 2001)

**Robin, Vicki, and Joe Dominguez,** *Your Money or Your Life* (Penguin, revised and updated edition, 2008)

**Schell, Jonathan,** *Fate of the Earth* (Knopf, 1982)

**Simmons, Matt,** *Twilight in the Desert: The Coming Saudi Oil Shock and the World Economy* (John Wiley & Sons, 2005)

**Smith, Huston,** *Cleansing the Doors of Perception: The Religious Significance of Entheogenic Plants and Chemicals* (Sentinel Publications, third edition, 2003)

**Solnit, Rebecca,** *A Paradise Built in Hell* (Viking Penguin, 2009)

**Tennison, Sharon,** *The Power of Impossible Ideas* (Oderwald Press, 2012)

**Tick, Ed,** *War and the Soul: Healing Our Nation's Veterans from Post-Traumatic Stress Disorder* (Quest Books, 2005) and more recently *Warrior's Return: Restoring the Soul After War* (Sounds True, 2014)

**Weller, Francis,** *The Wild Edge of Sorrow: Rituals of Renewal and the Sacred Work of Grief* (North Atlantic Books, 2015)

**Whyte, William Foote,** "Social Inventions for Solving Human Problems," *Clinical Sociology Review,* 5:1 (1987)

**Yaconelli, Mark Y.,** *The Gift of Hard Things: Finding Grace in Unexpected Places* (IVP Books, 2016)

# Original Publication or Broadcast

In alphabetical order, places of original publication or broadcast include *Alternet, The Huffington Post, Jefferson Monthly, Op Ed News,* and on Rogue Valley Community Television (RVTV). The majority of pieces, by far, were originally published by *The Huffington Post;* followed by those that RVTV broadcast.

Pieces that were picked up by a site called Resilience.org (maintained by the Post Carbon Institute) are indicated by a final R and include Chapters 5, 10, 20, 23, 26, 31, 32, 33, 35, 36, 37, 39, 40, 44.

Many articles were also linked on a daily news digest called "Speaking Truth to Power."

Most of the chapters in this book have appeared on the Internet. While the various sites received first serial rights, the author retains the copyright. I wish to thank the editors of these sites for their help. All titles that appeared on the articles are the same as listed in the table of contents of this book, unless indicated otherwise below.

### ALTERNET
Chapter 15b (for 15a see below, under *Op Ed News*): "Taking PTSD Seriously" on November 21, 2012, as "Research Points to Clear Benefits of MDMA for Post-Traumatic Stress Disorder"

### THE HUFFINGTON POST
Chapter 2: What's Your Story?, on February 4, 2013
Chapter 5: Abundance Gifting, on December 6, 2012; R
Chapter 8: Make Me Do It, on August 26, 2010
Chapter 9: The Power of Compassion, on December 14, 2015
Chapter 10: Transition Towns, on November 27, 2010 as "The Transition Town Movement's Initial Genius"; R
Chapter 16: The Sixties and Afterward, on May 5, 2010 as "Questions Coming Back to Life"
Chapter 17: Guided Psychedelic Sessions, on February 1, 2012
Chapter 19: Welcoming Warriors Home, on April 12, 2011
Chapter 20: Martin Luther King's Legacy, on January 21, 2013 as "Is MLK Of Use to Us Now?"; R
Chapter 21: John Monro's Mission, on December 28, 2012 as "Monro's Damage Control"
Chapter 22: Space Wealth, on April 24, 2012
Chapter 23: Economic Inequality, on March 28, 2011 as "After the American Dream"; R
Chapter 24: The Freedom of Simple Living, on November 8, 2013
Chapter 27: How Change Happened, on June 10, 2011

Chapter 28: Citizen Diplomacy, on October 17, 2012 as "When the People Lead, Leaders Will Follow"
Chapter 29: A Nuclear Secret, on June 20, 2010
Chapter 30: Out of Almost Everywhere, on September 7, 2010
Chapter 31: World on the Edge, on March 4, 2011; R
Chapter 32: The Global Crisis, on July 4, 2010 as "Inconvenient? You Ain't Seen Nothing Yet"; R
Chapter 33: A Suit for the Emperor, on November 26, 2012; R
Chapter 34: When Elites Fail, on May 20, 2011 as "Where Elites Fail"; R
Chapter 35: Our Renewable Future, on June 30, 2016; R
Chapter 36: Who's Got the Social Inventions?, on March 1, 2013; R
Chapter 37: Liberty Bonds: Bringing Ordinary People into the Energy Transition on August 22, 2016
Chapter 38: Perils of Geoengineering, on May 24, 2010 as "Hack the Planet?"
Chapter 39: Chilling Out Globally, on April 2, 2013; R
Chapter 40: Transform While There's Still Time, on December 2, 2013; R
Chapter 41: A Feminist Treasure, on January 11, 2012
Chapter 42: The Making of a Teacher, on February 13, 2012
Chapter 43: Remembering a Buddhist Psychotherapy Pioneer, on January 21, 2011
Chapter 44: A Vision of Life Beyond Consumerism, on October 25, 2010; R

*JEFFERSON MONTHLY* (a print magazine)
Chapter 26: Tilling Our Own Soil, in the March 2007 issue; R

*OP ED NEWS*
Chapter 1: The Grace of Social Inventions, on February 3, 2016
Chapter 14: From Loss to Joy, on June 19, 2015
Chapter 15a: Taking PTSD Seriously, on November 3, 2014
Chapter 18: Manifesting Minds on January 19, 2014 as "Mindful Molecules"

*ROGUE VALLEY COMMUNITY TELEVISION*
(on *Like, Wow!*, an interview show produced and hosted by the author)
Chapter 3: Baby Bonding for Dads
Chapter 4: A Center for Artists
Chapter 6: Learning for Elders
Chapter 7: New Tribes
Chapter 11: The Mankind Project
Chapter 12: Mentoring in the Rose Circle
Chapter 13: Boys to Men
Chapter 22: Space Wealth
Chapter 25: Back to the Farm

# Acknowledgements

First of all I want to thank the editors of the Internet websites that published many of what have become chapters in this book, especially the "blogteam" at *The Huffington Post*. I once overheard a friend of my wife ask her, "How big is Craig's audience on *HuffPo*?" She was told it's somewhere between the millions of unique monthly visitors claimed by the site and a few friends—in that range. I also want to thank all the sources for those articles and the people described in them.

With regard to production of this book, I am most grateful to the talented people with whom I worked on earlier books in this trilogy, in particular Deborah Mokma, the copyeditor, and Chris Molé, designer at Book Savvy Studio in Ashland. Chris is also the designer of other books for Willow Press.

In terms of publication, this book grew out of a piece that I wrote in 2007 for *Sentient Times*, a brilliant periodical then edited and published by Deborah Mokma and distributed throughout what we call the State of Jefferson, which includes the far north of California and much of western Oregon. The article was about "social capital" and it described some community-building projects that figure, at greater length, in chapters of this book.

Chris not only designed three magnificent covers for The Gratitude Trilogy, but also laid out the interior of the books. She then oversaw production for Willow Press. Like Deborah, Chris was fun to work with and discerning about the presentation of the argument, both in words and in format.

# About the Author

A graduate of Harvard College, editor of *The Harvard Crimson* there, winner of the Frank Knox Fellowship for study abroad, Craig K. Comstock has worked mainly as co-director of the William James Center in Berkeley, then as a book creation coach with private clients, and also, for five years, as director of the Ark Foundation. After an adulthood largely in the San Francisco Bay Area, he now lives in Southern Oregon, where he produced and hosted a weekly TV show on "people doing admirable things" and writes extensively for the Internet. Author of several published books, he completed *Gift of Darkness: Growing Up in Occupied Amsterdam* in 2015, and *Enlarging Our Comfort Zones* in 2016.

www.ingramcontent.com/pod-product-compliance
Lightning Source LLC
Chambersburg PA
CBHW062049270326
41931CB00013B/3001